Mother

Goose

Time

Mother Goose Time

Library Programs for Babies and Their Caregivers

by Jane Marino and Dorothy F. Houlihan

Music Arrangements by Jane Marino
Photographs by Susan G. Drinker

The H. W. Wilson Company
1992

Marino, Jane.
   Mother Goose time : library programs for babies and their
caregivers / by Jane Marino and Dorothy F. Houlihan ; photographs by
Susan G. Drinker.
    p. cm.
   Includes bibliographical references and index.
   ISBN 0-8242-0850-1
   1. Libraries. Children's—Activity programs. 2. Babysitters—
Services for. 3. Infants—Services for. I. Houlihan, Dorothy F.
II. Title.
Z718.1.M277 1992
027.62'5—dc20   91-46986

Printed in the United States of America
First Printing

To my mother, Mildred Moran Keegan,
for sharing her love of music.
And to my father, Eugene Keegan,
for sharing his love of words.

—JM

To my mother, Maureen Sullivan Fearn,
and my grandmothers, whose voices echo through
the pages of this book.

—DFH

Contents

Foreword   ix

Acknowledgments   xi

Part I: Introducing Mother Goose

What Is Mother Goose Time?   1
  You and Mother Goose Time   2
  The Evolution of the Program: Mother Goose Grows Up   5
Planning   12
  Getting Started   12
Preparation   15
  Material Selection   15
  Advertisement   22
  Registration   23
  Rehearsal   25
Program   28
  Greeting   28
  Transition to Programming Area   30
  Leading the Program   30
  Closing   34
  Contingencies   36
Evaluation   37
One Final Word   38

Part II: Rhymes and Songs

Types of Rhymes and Songs   41
Lap   41
Imitation   70
Activity   89

Part III: Resources

Evaluation Form for Mother Goose 105
Music Appendix 107
Display Books 123
Suggested Picture-Book Titles for Mother Goose Time 127
Resource Books 131
Rhyme Indexes 137
    Title Index of All Rhymes and Songs 139
    Title Index of Spoken Rhymes 145
    Title Index of Sung Rhymes 149
    Title Index of Rhymes by Developmental Levels 153
    Lap Rhymes, Prewalkers 153
    Lap Rhymes, Both Groups 155
    Imitation Rhymes, Walkers 159
    Imitation Rhymes, Both Groups 161
    Activity Rhymes, Walkers 163
    Activity Rhymes, Both Groups 165
    First Line Index of All Rhymes 167

Foreword

Infant programming is relatively new in public library circles and this book will serve as a guide and catalyst for helping children's librarians to program to this population.

In order to achieve the communication skills that are essential in life, a baby has to climb many language steps—listening, imitating sounds, talking, transferring sounds to written symbols and finally reading. The learning process is done by layering and linking more information onto an existing base of knowledge. We learn to listen, in order to listen to learn. As keepers and disseminators of the language in literature, children's librarians have indispensable roles in the task of giving these language steps to infants and their caregivers.

The definite rhythm, brevity, repetition and dramatic imagery of nursery rhymes and finger games make them the most satisfying literature to use for this task. By using rhymes in a multi-sensory experience, the spirit and intention of this oral traditional literature is kept alive. The melody and cadence of the English language are correctly experienced in the activities of sound and motion which can be found in the material selected here. They will help the librarian and caregivers sing, speak, and saturate the infants in their care with well ordered, well chosen words from the best in this genre of literature so that the language process can begin.

First impressions of language, as other things in life, are lasting. The echoes of our childhood will be heard all our lives. Adults who give those first impressions must be sure the echoes will be beautiful and appropriate. This book will help make that so.

Sandra Stroner Sivulich
1992

Acknowledgments

This book was inspired by a program originated by two librarians whose enthusiasm and experience gave Mother Goose Time its start and whose dedication kept it going. We would therefore like to thank Sandra Sivulich and Barbara Ginsberg for their love and support during our years with this program and during the creation and writing of this book. We have been fortunate to work for a library supportive of our professional endeavors and we would like to acknowledge the administration and staff of the White Plains Public Library for their encouragement with this project. We have also been blessed with husbands and children whose unending love, patience, and forbearance have allowed us to focus on this undertaking. But most of all, we want to remember and thank all the babies and their adults who have brightened our programs with their smiles and songs and who have given back to us more than we could ever give them.

The authors are grateful for permission to include:

"Arms High, Arms Low" ("Yankee Doodle Exercise") from *Baby Games*, a recording created by Priscilla Hegner with musical arrangements by Dennis Buck. Copyright © 1987 Kimbo Educational. Used by permission of Kimbo Educational.

"Baby A Go Go" from *The Baby Record Featuring Bob McGrath and Katharine Smithrim*. Copyright © 1983 Western Publishing (Canada), Inc. Used by permission.

"Baby Grows" ("Five Little Fingers") from *Toddlers on Parade: Musical Exercises for Infants and Toddlers*, a recording created by Carol Hammett and Elaine Bueffel with musical arrangements by Dennis Buck. Copyright © 1985 Kimbo Educational. Used by permission of Kimbo Educational.

"Bees Don't Care about the Snow" ("Bees Do Not Like the Snow") by Frank Dempster Sherman from *Pinafore Palace*, edited by Kate Douglas Wiggin and Nora Archibald Smith. Published by Doubleday, Doran, & Co., 1907.

"Bluebirds" ("Two Little Blackbirds") musical arrangement from *The Eentsy, Weentsy Spider: Fingerplays and Action Rhymes*, compiled by Joanna Cole and Stephanie Calmenson. Text copyright © 1991 by Joanna Cole and Stephanie Calmenson. Reprinted by permission of Morrow Junior Books, a division of Morrow Books, Inc.

"Clap Your Hands Little Sally" ("Little Baby Dear") from *The Baby Record Featuring Bob McGrath and Katharine Smithrim.* Copyright © 1983 Western Publishing (Canada), Inc. Used by permission.

"Come A Look A See" from *The Baby Record Featuring Bob McGrath and Katharine Smithrim.* Copyright © 1983 Western Publishing (Canada), Inc. Used by permission.

"Eins, Zwei/One, Two" ("A German Game") from *Rhymes for Learning Times* by Louise Binder Scott. Copyright © 1983. Published by T. S. Denison & Co., Inc., Minneapolis, Minnesota. Used by permission of publisher.

"Fee, Fie, Foe, Fum" reprinted from *Ring a Ring O'Roses,* published by the Flint Public Library, Flint, Michigan. (313) 232-7111.

"The Flower" ("Green Leaf") reprinted from *Ring a Ring O'Roses,* published by the Flint Public Library, Flint, Michigan. (313) 232-7111.

"Gently Falling Leaves" ("Little Leaves") reprinted from *Ring a Ring O'Roses,* published by the Flint Public Library, Flint, Michigan. (313) 232-7111.

"Hand to Knee Stretch" ("Mary Had a Little Lamb Exercise") from *Baby Games,* a recording created by Priscilla Hegner with musical arrangements by Dennis Buck. Copyright © 1987 Kimbo Educational. Used by permission of Kimbo Educational.

"Hello" ("Hello II"), words and music by Ella Jenkins from *The Ella Jenkins Song Book for Children,* created by Ella Jenkins. Copyright © Ell-Bern, 1966. Used by permission of author.

"If" ("If Your Fingers") reprinted from *Ring a Ring O'Roses,* published by the Flint Public Library, Flint, Michigan. (313) 232-7111.

"I Have a Little Heart" reprinted with permission of the American Library Association from *Storytimes for Two-Year-Olds* by Judy Nichols, © 1987 by the American Library Association.

"I Have a Nose" ("Myself") reprinted with permission of the American Library Association from *Storytimes for Two-Year-Olds* by Judy Nichols, © 1987 by the American Library Association.

"I'm Growing" reprinted from *Ring a Ring O'Roses,* published by the Flint Public Library, Flint, Michigan. (313) 232-7111.

"I Put My Arms Up High" reprinted from *Ring a Ring O'Roses,* published by the Flint Public Library, Flint, Michigan. (313) 232-7111.

"I Wiggle" ("I Wiggle My Fingers") by Lucille F. Wood and Louise Binder Scott from *Rhymes for Fingers and Flannelboards* by Louise Binder Scott and J. J. Thompson. Used by permission of T. S. Denison & Co., Minneapolis, Minnesota.

"Jack-O-Lantern" reprinted with permission of the American Library Association from *Storytimes for Two-Year-Olds* by Judy Nichols, © 1987 by the American Library Association.

"A Japanese Game" from *Rhymes for Learning Times* by Louise Binder Scott. Copyright © 1983. Published by T. S. Denison & Co., Inc., Minneapolis, Minnesota. Used by permission of publisher.

"Legs Up, Boo" ("One Potato") from *Baby Games,* a recording created by Priscilla Hegner with musical arrangements by Dennis Buck. Copyright © 1987 Kimbo Educational. Used by permission of Kimbo Educational.

"Little Rabbit" ("I Saw a Little Rabbit") reprinted with permission of the American Library Association from *Storytimes for Two-Year-Olds* by Judy Nichols, © 1987 by the American Library Association.

"Mix a Pancake" from *Sing-Song* by Christina G. Rossetti (New York: MacMillan, 1924).

"Mother and Father and Uncle John" from *The Baby Record Featuring Bob McGrath and Katharine Smithrim*. Copyright © 1983 Western Publishing (Canada), Inc. Used by permission.

"My Eyes Can See" reprinted from *Ring a Ring O'Roses*, published by the Flint Public Library, Flint, Michigan. (313) 232-7111.

"My Garden" ("This Is My Garden" reprinted with permission of the American Library Association from *Storytimes for Two-Year-Olds* by Judy Nichols, © 1987 by the American Library Association.

"My Hands" ("Thank You Rhyme") reprinted from *Ring a Ring O'Roses*, published by the Flint Public Library, Flint, Michigan. (313) 232-7111.

"Old Mother Goose" from *The Mother Goose Songbook* by Tom Glazer, illustrated by David McPhail. Copyright piano arrangements, original words and music and adaptations of traditional words and music © 1990 by Tom Glazer, Songs Music Inc. Used by permission of Doubleday, a division of Bantam Doubleday Dell Publishing Group, Inc.

"Pitter Patter" reprinted from *Ring a Ring O'Roses*, published by the Flint Public Library, Flint, Michigan. (313) 232-7111.

"Reach for the Ceiling" ("Touch Your Head") reprinted from *Ring a Ring O'Roses*, published by the Flint Public Library, Flint, Michigan. (313) 232-7111.

"Rickety, Rickety Rocking Horse" from *The Baby Record Featuring Bob McGrath and Katharine Smithrim*. Copyright © 1983 Western Publishing (Canada), Inc. Used by permission.

"Rima de Chocolate" ("Spanish Chocolate Rhyme") from *Tortillitas Para Mama and Other Nursery Rhymes Spanish and English*, selected and translated by Margot C. Griego, Betsy L. Bucks, Sharon S. Gilbert and Laurel H. Kimball. Copyright © 1981 by Margot Griego, Betsy Bucks, Sharon Gilbert and Laurel Kimball. Reprinted by permission of Henry Holt and Company, Inc.

"Roll Your Hands" from *Toddlers on Parade: Musical Exercises for Infants and Toddlers*, a recording created by Carol Hammett and Elain Bueffel with musical arrangements by Dennis Buck. Copyright © 1985 Kimbo Educational. Used by permission of Kimbo Educational.

"Safety" ("Stoplight") reprinted from *Ring a Ring O'Roses*, published by the Flint Public Library, Flint, Michigan. (313) 232-7111.

"Say, Say Oh Baby" ("Oh Baby") from *Baby Games*, a recording created by Priscilla Hegner with musical arrangements by Dennis Buck. Copyright © 1987 Kimbo Educational. Used by permission of Kimbo Educational.

"Snowboys" from *Paper Stories* by Jean Stangl. 1984 © Fearon Teacher Aids, PO Box 280, Carthage, Illinois 62321. Used by permission.

"The Snowman" reprinted from *Ring a Ring O'Roses*, published by the Flint Public Library, Flint, Michigan. (313) 232-7111.

"These Are Baby's Fingers" from *The Baby Record Featuring Bob McGrath and Katharine Smithrim*. Copyright © 1983 Western Publishing (Canada), Inc. Used by permission.

"Tommy O'Flynn" from *The Baby Record Featuring Bob McGrath and Katharine Smithrim*. Copyright © 1983 Western Publishing (Canada), Inc. Used by permission.

"Sometimes I Am Tall" reprinted from *Ring a Ring O'Roses*, published by the Flint Public Library, Flint, Michigan. (313) 232-7111.

"Ten Little Fingers" ("I Have Ten Fingers") reprinted from *Ring a Ring O'Roses*, published by the Flint Public Library, Flint, Michigan. (313) 232-7111.

"To Market, To Market" from *The Mother Goose Songbook* by Tom Glazer, illustrated by David McPhail. Copyright piano arrangements, original words and music and adaptations of traditional words and music © 1990 by Tom Glazer, Songs Music Inc. Used by permission of Doubleday, a division of Bantam Doubleday Dell Publishing Group, Inc.

"Touch" ("Quiet Time Rhyme") reprinted from *Ring a Ring O'Roses*, published by the Flint Public Library, Flint, Michigan. (313) 232-7111.

"Touch Your Nose" reprinted from *Ring a Ring O'Roses*, published by the Flint Public Library, Flint, Michigan. (313) 232-7111.

"Two Little" ("Two Little Feet") reprinted from *Ring a Ring O'Roses*, published by the Flint Public Library, Flint, Michigan. (313) 232-7111.

"Valentines" reprinted from *Ring a Ring O'Roses*, published by the Flint Public Library, Flint, Michigan. (313) 232-7111.

"What Am I?" ("Jack-O-Lantern II") reprinted from *Ring a Ring O'Roses*, published by the Flint Public Library, Flint, Michigan. (313) 232-7111.

"What Are You Wearing?" reprinted with permission of the American Library Association from *Storytimes for Two-Year-Olds* by Judy Nichols, © 1987 by the American Library Association.

"Wiggle" ("Wiggle, Wiggle Fingers") reprinted from *Ring a Ring O'Roses*, published by the Flint Public Library, Flint, Michigan. (313) 232-7111.

PART I

INTRODUCING MOTHER GOOSE TIME

What is Mother Goose Time?

Mother Goose Time is a library program in which short rhymes, songs, finger plays, and books are combined in a gentle and intimate program for babies and their caregivers. But even more than that, it is an invitation to all to enter a wonderful world filled with songs and rhymes, clapping hands and smiling faces, wide eyes and comfortable laps. This is the world started with Mother Goose rhymes and continued by people who use these rhymes to shower babies with the soft and gentle rain of wonderful words and gentle tunes. This shower will help those babies grow into bright, inquisitive toddlers and children eager to learn.

You and Mother Goose Time

You need only to work with very young children as a children's librarian or professional to become a part of this wonderful world. Consider this book your invitation. You have a unique opportunity not only to connect with children from the beginning of their lives but with their parents and caregivers as well. By establishing and conducting a program exclusively for babies, you demonstrate to their adults how important they and their children are to you and the public library.

Many adults whose use of public libraries stopped after their own school years return to the public library only after becoming parents. Welcome their babies. "Capture them in the cradle" with a program aimed just at babies, and right from the start you will demonstrate that the library is a place for children. Such a program will be their children's first impression of all the library has to offer, and every time their adults bring them into the library, it will be more than a place with books, tables, and tapes. They will recognize the library as the wonder-filled place where they sing and clap hands. And they will connect with you as the person who sings and claps with them.

This is an interactive program: you are not performing but rather sharing rhymes and songs with the babies and adults who come to your program. And at times they are sharing theirs with you! But you are doing something even more important. You are giving them words and images from wonderful literature so their language process can begin. You are establishing the connection between them and the books that have these rhymes and the rhymes themselves. You are helping to foster a new generation of readers.

A lasting impression made on the littlest library user to establish a life-long library habit is not the least of the benefits from a program for infants. The program described in this book is a language-enrichment program. It helps a child learn how to listen. It introduces the babies to and reminds their caregivers of the beautiful words and soothing rhymes from generations of literature. Listening to those words spoken and sung in a comfortable atmosphere and reinforced at home can be a valuable guidepost along the road to speaking and, eventually, reading.

As babies listen, they will involve their entire bodies, whether they are infants kicking their legs and clasping their fingers while cooing back at the adult face singing to them or toddlers reaching up or clapping their hands on their own. Clapping, tapping, reaching, and rocking are all physical reinforcements of the rhymes used and can trigger later recall of the words outside the program. Many mothers have told us about their children's favorite rhymes, like 1½-year-old Joseph who would walk into the library and immediately lift his arms over his head—mimicking the movement for our "Exercises" chant with which we begin every program. And 15-month-old Abigail, according to her mother, rolls her hands around and around at the mention of Mother Goose Time, just as we do when we sing "The Wheels on the Bus."

In the same way, the rhythm and cadence of the words help reinforce the listening process. Kathleen, who first came to Mother Goose Time when she was 7 months old, provides a perfect example of each child's unique listening process. For over a year, she came with her father to every month's program, content to sit on his lap and watch us. He assured us that Kathleen enjoyed herself and "talked" about Mother Goose Time at home, even though she seemed uninvolved while she was here. Then, one day, after months of limited response, she blossomed into the biggest fan of Mother Goose Time, singing, clapping, and moving along with us. Unlike some children who respond immediately, Kathleen's listening and learning process was gradual, almost as though she were hoarding her response until she had it all down. Only then was she able to let loose and fully respond.

Spoken or sung, what is important is not the tune but the nature of rhymes. Singing or chanting the rhymes will help you and the babies remember the words, in the same way that the accompanying actions reinforce the lyrics. The actual tune used is not important; in fact, one librarian we know sings every nursery rhyme to the tune of "Frere Jacques." But it works for her, so it works for the babies who are listening. The babies will think you sound beautiful, even if you don't—or even if you only know one tune!

This program is called Mother Goose Time more in consideration of the state of mind that is created than due to the specific rhymes we

use. The rhymes in this book go way beyond the realm of those considered traditional Mother Goose and have been collected from a variety of sources, including our own childhoods. You may recognize many of them. Others have been adapted or changed—sometimes to suit our personalities, sometimes to suit the babies we've met in our programs. But no matter what you call this program, which of the rhymes you use, or how you change them to suit *your* needs, remember that your program will work because the rhymes can be readily incorporated into babies' everyday lives. Short, memorable, and portable, nursery rhymes are easily digestible entertainment and stimulation that match a baby's attention span. All you have to do is get the ball rolling. Once you do, this book can be your support when you have none, your partner when you are all by yourself, and your creative energy when you've run out. Join us in this world and discover how really wonderful it is.

The Evolution of the Program: Mother Goose Grows Up

This book offers two valuable resources: rhymes that work with very young children and the context, or program, in which we have found these rhymes to be the most effective. In order to best present that context, we thought a brief history and description of our program would be in order.

Our library has offered a program for very young children for over ten years. At its inception, library programming for babies was itself in its infancy and our predecessors were faced with the prospect of "inventing the wheel." But enthusiasm for and a commitment to early childhood programming overcame the lack of available resources, and "Mother Goose Time" was born. Experienced with children's literature, the librarians who began the program found that appropriate material for very young children consisted of traditional nursery rhymes and songs. But since the use of this material in a library setting was groundbreaking, no framework existed for bringing these rhymes out of the nursery and into the library. So when Mother Goose Time began, it bore a marked resemblance to existing, traditional preschool library programming. The librarians used an overriding thematic structure that incorporated props and scripts, while an auditorium-style room arrangement created a clear physical separation between the programmers and the audience.

Despite the program's traditional framework, its attempt to reach

such a young audience was innovative. Many libraries, including our own, had already successfully expanded their preschool programming to include a program for toddlers aged approximately 2½ to 3½ years. But few had ventured into the uncharted territory of the very young—the under 2½'s. A fortuitous combination of intuition, courage, and serendipity told those pioneering librarians that if you could successfully program to toddlers, there was nothing to stop you from programming to even younger children, even those as young as 6 months to 2½ years.

Recognition of the wide age range in this audience led to the creation of two separate registration groups, 6 months to 18 months and 19 months to 2½ years. The two groups divided neatly into a 12-month span for each, while also giving a nod to the difference in abilities between the two groups. However, with a scripted, thematic format, the program to which both groups were exposed was essentially the same. Although the physical separation between the programmers and the group prevented a totally interactive experience, an effort was made to encourage participants to continue the rhymes at home by handing out scripts to them.

The novelty of the program, and its ability to fill a programming need not previously met, together with the dynamic creativity of the people who were working with a new age group, gave Mother Goose Time the momentum to successfully carry it through the first few years. When its originators moved on to other jobs, we took over the programming of Mother Goose. Since this was a new program for us, albeit one already in place for our library, we had a unique opportunity to look at it with fresh eyes.

Through a gradual process, we began a series of small but significant changes that led to the existing program. Working with the program in its original form, we came to fully understand that programming to a child before he or she can talk is also aimed at the adult who brings the child to the library. Since we would never advise that a new parent wait to sing or read to their baby until the child was 6 months old, it didn't seem logical to impose an arbitrary minimum age for a program intended to introduce their children to the joy of sharing language and literature. By opening the program up to babies from birth, we hoped to send a strong message to parents that they and their children, no matter what age, are valued and welcome in the library.

Expanding the age range, however, gave us too wide a range of developmental abilities in the younger group. We had added babies who, it seemed, would have limited immediate response into a group which already had babies old enough to walk, talk, and sing along but who, we firmly believed, would benefit from listening to nursery rhymes at Mother Goose Time. However, rhymes with enough action to engage 18-month old babies would leave out the very young infants, while gentler, and sometimes, slower rhymes, perfect for newborns, might bore the older, more mobile babies.

One solution, startling to us in its simplicity, was to divide the children along their developmental abilities. Instead of the more traditional chronological-age labeling, we began identifying each group according to what they were able to do. Thus, we called new-born infants "Lap Babies," indicating their limited physical mobility; more active babies able to get around became known as "Crawlers"; and the group with the greatest physical independence were called "Walkers."

Although these three labels made perfect sense to us, this breakdown met with limited success. Staff and parents found the revised labeling system cumbersome during registration. Differentiating between "lap babies" and "crawlers" meant splitting developmental hairs. We realized that the same rhymes could work for all babies who were not yet walking, whether they were sitting on laps or crawling around on the floor. Thus, the younger developmental group became known simply as "Prewalkers," the older group as "Walkers." That this was immediately comprehensible to registering parents confirmed its practicability for us.

This new emphasis on developmental level rather than age also gave us the opportunity to assess the rhymes and songs as well as the manner in which we presented them. The more we worked with babies, the more apparent it became that in their small and immediate world the person singing or speaking to them should be close and immediate. Sitting on chairs in front of the group created both a physical and psychological distance, and we needed to establish an intimacy that had not previously existed. To be ten feet away from a baby is to be out of its world.

One thing that helped span the distance between the babies and us was reading a picture book to the group. This proved a powerful device for capturing their attention regardless of their distance from us. Opening a book was a magical moment. Every baby stopped to

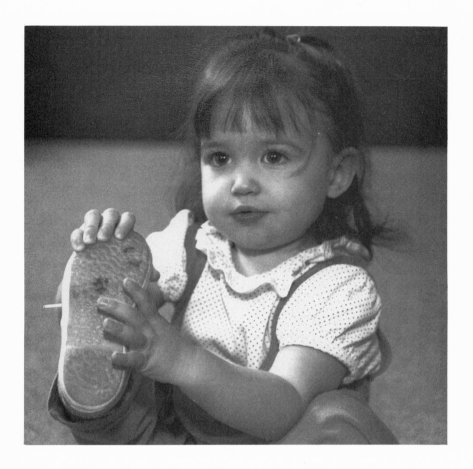

listen and to look. Another attempt at establishing intimacy was made by asking that everyone introduce themselves and their babies, but in such a spread out, static group—with adults and babies lined up in rows on the floor at our feet—knowing their names did not really change the atmosphere of the program. Anonymity was not creating the problem; rather, our physical arrangement itself established an artificial distance. So we got off our chairs and onto carpet squares; out of rows and into a circle.

In this new, intimate setting, the props and scripts we had used proved more obstacle than aid. We needed a gentler, more spontaneous and flexible style of programming with rhymes and songs that parents could use outside the program. We felt able to go beyond the confines of a thematic program that had no transference to "the real world" and which meant nothing to babies anyway. We stopped using esoteric, theme-oriented original verse and swung back to the more universal, recognizable, traditional rhymes. Parents found that, because they could identify more of the rhymes we used, they were easier to remember. We no longer needed to hand out scripts to the adults, and they stopped worrying about following along with the script and were able to simply enjoy Mother Goose Time, saying or singing the rhymes with their children. We were no longer performing; we were sharing.

Realizing that we still needed a prompt of some kind but finding the scripts cumbersome and awkward, we prepared 4 × 6 index cards with the rhymes or songs that we planned to use in our programs to cue us. They eliminated the worry that we would forget what verse we wanted to do or forget the words to the verse.

As we became more committed to the concept of a developmental division, many of the rhymes we had previously used became unworkable, especially those with a strong thematic orientation. Unable to simply transfer the old rhyme collection onto index cards and use them indiscriminately, we needed to reevaluate them in terms of our new program.

A period of trial and error revealed the simple truth: all nursery rhymes are not created equal. While extensively published in collection and picture-book form, nursery rhymes have, with few exceptions, no specific instructions on use with an infant, other than to read it to them. Nor do they have a developmental focus. Some rhymes are wonderful for babies to grow with and can be used from the time they are born until they are too old for this type of program. Others, however, require a level of activity or comprehension that make them appropriate for one developmental level and unsuitable for another.

By selecting rhymes from collections and field-testing them in the program with actual babies, we were able to give the rhymes a developmental focus, matching appropriate rhymes to developmental ages. We discovered what worked for Prewalkers, what engaged Walkers, and even, since some rhymes are not age-specific, which rhymes satisfied the program's entire developmental age range.

Once we recognized those differences, we needed the rhymes to reflect the possible levels of activity as used with each group; thus the labels "Lap," "Imitation," and "Activity" evolved. Lap rhymes have almost no accompanying physical activity. Many of the more traditional Mother Goose rhymes fall into this category. Imitation rhymes introduce a moderate level of action, such as pointing at oneself or other things around you or even just clapping hands. Activity rhymes usually involve the whole body with actions like walking, jumping, or turning around. So each rhyme is identified here in two ways: by developmental level and by activity level.

Here's an example. A longer song like "The Wheels on the Bus" is an imitation song that works with older babies—Walkers—who can roll and clap hands, but not with Prewalkers who cannot do these things and will quickly lose interest. Better to use a lap rhyme like "Ride a Cock Horse" that requires nothing more of Prewalkers than to sit on a pair of galloping knees and enjoy the rhythm of the song.

This developmental and activity focus makes it possible to take still other rhymes, such as "The Noble Duke of York," and flex them to grow with the babies. For the Prewalkers, it is a "flying-baby song" as the adults lift their babies "up" and "down" on the appropriate words. For the Walkers, it is a whole-body activity as we all stand up and encourage both adults and children to raise and lower their arms on the appropriate words.

So, armed with index cards, appropriately labeled rhymes, eager babies and caregivers, we will take you through a program such as the one we have been using and envision for your use. Imagine, if you will, approximately ten to fifteen babies and their caregivers gathering into a circle on the floor. The adults are sitting on carpet squares; the babies are on their laps or seated before them, looking to the programmers for the program to begin.

We start the same way every time: by introducing Mother Goose Time as a language-enrichment program. For the benefit of newcomers and as a reminder to returning participants, we explain that we will share rhymes, songs, finger plays, and books with the adults and their babies in the hope that they continue to share and enjoy these rhymes and books at home.

We then invite the grown-ups to introduce themselves and the babies they have brought with them (including older siblings), and

we introduce ourselves. We start with the same song or couple of songs every month, giving the participants a wonderful feeling of recognition and the program a sense of continuity. We then do anywhere from ten to twelve rhymes and songs, with varied activity levels, lasting anywhere from fifteen to twenty minutes. Next, we read a book to the group, then sing a lullaby to them, thank everyone for coming, and do a good-bye rhyme which signals the program's end. Many times, participants will linger as the babies play with one another and the caregivers have a chance to chat, but eventually they drift out, making room for the next group to enter. Sounds simple, doesn't it? It can be, with the proper planning and preparation.

Planning

Getting Started

Although Mother Goose Time programming may now sound like a good idea to you, it will probably be necessary for you to evaluate the

program in terms of your specific circumstances. You should first determine how it can fit into your overall programming plan by asking yourself certain specific questions.

(1) Why? This is probably the most important question. Once you have answered it and are comfortable with the answer, you can convince not only those in charge at your library but also your public

how invaluable the program is. In finding your own answer, some of the important goals to keep in mind for such a program are:

—To bring babies into the library so that you can introduce them and their caregivers to the wonderful literature that awaits them.

—To demonstrate the importance and value of this age group in and of itself, and as a part of the library's public.

—To give parents and babies the opportunity and ability to share rhymes and songs both within the context of the program and outside the library.

—To establish and foster a life-long library habit.

—To build a rapport with the parents, some of whom are new library users, that they will appreciate and remember, bringing them back not just to this program but to the library, again and again.

(2) Who? In other words, for whom are you programming? Are you seeing parents and caregivers of new-born children coming into your library? Do you have a young population? Are you getting requests from parents to do programs for children younger than those in your current repertoire? Do you have a successful, ongoing pre-school or toddler program? If you have answered yes to any of these questions, a Mother Goose Time program will work for you. Although the age span for this program is large, from birth to toddlerhood, you can start with a small segment of that stretch, if you need to, and expand slowly to include all the ages. If that means starting with Walkers, for example, to get a feel for the program and the rhymes in it, remember it's still a start—a good start.

(3) What? This is a language-enrichment program for babies from the very beginning of their lives. Please forget all the traditional storytimes that have gone before. They are not the same.

(4) When? Even if you're now motivated to do this program, you must make decisions on how it will fit into your schedule, unless you have unlimited staff and personnel dollars. You need time to plan and prepare for it, not to mention the hours spent actually programming. In all likelihood, the activity level in your library will rise as a result of this program, and you need to take into account the additional impact on your circulation and shelving staff.

Compare your current programming schedule to the existing staff schedule. Poll the parents who come into the library regarding what times might work for them—mornings, afternoons, early evenings? Weekdays or weekends? Keep in mind that naptimes and feedings are a major consideration, but be realistic in fitting requested program times and days into your own schedule.

(5) Where? A special place must be established for this program. Look beyond your traditional locations. If the children's programming room, the auditorium, or the community room doesn't provide the intimacy and atmosphere conducive to a program for babies, look around and choose another spot. It doesn't have to be a big place or uniquely decorated for infants. But the area should be as clear as possible of distractions or dangers. Since babies tend to accept library books on shelves as an intrinsic part of a library, rather than seeing them as obvious playthings, don't worry if your programming space is actually in your picture-book area. But no matter where you choose, it will work if it has the right atmosphere—an atmosphere that will be created mainly by you.

Preparation

Material Selection

This book will provide you with over 150 baby-tested and toddler-approved rhymes to use in your program. What was it about these rhymes that gave them the babies' seal of approval? The rhymes, in the time-tested oral tradition of Mother Goose rhymes, share a delicious language infused with inherent rhythm and natural cadence. It's not important whether the language paints a vivid picture the way it does in "Ride a Cock Horse" or simply strings together staccato syllables as in "Baby A-Go Go," because the effect is the same: delighted babies.

The universal appeal and transferability of the wide range of rhymes and songs included here allow them to work in any setting. What has worked in the nursery for generations of parents can be just as effective in the library for new generations of librarians. Working their magic in your program, these rhymes will be brought home from the library in the minds and the hearts of the babies and their caregivers. They will be eager to share them again, allowing the rhymes to travel a full and natural circle: from the nursery, to the library, and back home again.

All the rhymes are effective, however different their functions may be: a lullaby soothes; a finger game amuses; and an activity rhyme distracts. With that in mind, the rhymes in this book have been grouped into a "Lap" section, an "Imitation" section, and an "Activity" section. While the various rhymes in each section are designated as useful for Walkers, Prewalkers, or both groups, an index at the back of the book will help you find those rhymes specifically geared to the developmental level you aim to reach.

But this doesn't tell you how or where to begin. Before you can pick the right rhymes, you have to know who will be listening to them. If you have decided to do a program for Walkers, for example, you can concentrate on those rhymes. If you've decided to do both a Walker and Prewalker group, you haven't necessarily doubled your work load, because you can choose many rhymes that will work for both groups, saving yourself time.

Since the best place to begin choosing rhymes is with the things you know, first look through the rhymes for any you might recognize. If you recognize lots of rhymes—great! Mother Goose is in your blood and soon you'll be on your way to a successful program. Don't be alarmed, however, if you don't recognize many rhymes. Even if this is the first time you've seen most of these rhymes, you can still find many you will like and can use in a program. Take your time, read the rhymes aloud, and attempt the actions which accompany the rhymes, if there are any. This is the only sure method to determine which sound good to you and suit your personality. Do the sounds delight your ear and tickle your tongue? Is the rhyme of manageable length and memorable imagery? Do you like it?

Two of the things to look for in a rhyme are the length and rhythm that work best for you. If you're new at this, it might be best to start with rhymes that are both short and snappy, because if you have trouble saying them, you'll have trouble remembering them. Even if you think you're tone deaf, don't shy away from the rhymes for which we have provided music. Just because we've suggested a melody for a rhyme doesn't mean you *must* sing it. Many of the "sung" rhymes, especially the short ones, are just as successful when they are spoken. They have natural cadences that give them a sing/song quality without your needing to rely on the actual tune. A rhyme that clearly demonstrates how easily this can work is "Open,

Shut Them." An old favorite that many librarians have used success-fully as a spoken rhyme, it also has a traditional tune that can make it an easy, cheerful song. So try it either way. Conversely, if you want to sing a rhyme that we have labeled as "spoken," sing away—by all means!

As you put your program together, pick several rhymes from each of the activity-level sections that appeal to you and with which you feel comfortable when you test them aloud. With any luck at all, you will have found enough rhymes to constitute your first program. How many is enough? Since each rhyme will be said at least twice, and allowing for liberal applause between takes, ten to twelve rhymes should be sufficient to complete a twenty-minute program. But al-ways have an additional three to five rhymes with you in case of last-minute substitutions. More about that later. The ten to twelve rhymes comprise the bulk of your program, and while you may sub-stitute or introduce some new rhymes for each subsequent program, it is important to have the same opening and closing rhymes to establish a routine which your babies and adults will come to recog-nize and expect. We've given you "hello songs" and "thank you" or "good-bye" rhymes and your choice of these or any other favorite rhymes will become your own opening and closing signatures.

Though you may bravely choose to try some new rhymes each program, always carry over a few of the more successful rhymes from previous sessions. The adults in your program will be grateful, be-cause the more you repeat, the more rhymes they will be comfortable with and the more likely they will be to do them at home. And the easier it will be for you to learn the rhymes and say them with confi-dence.

We usually do five or six of the same rhymes for several con-secutive sessions, until they become so old hat, that it's time to drop them off the roster. Yet, having a certain number of old favorites allows you to introduce more challenging rhymes with a minimum of resistance. We've had luck incorporating foreign-language rhymes as long as we've been careful to surround them with familiar, comfort-able rhymes.

This is not to say that the best-laid plans won't backfire. Despite careful, thoughtful preparation and practice, you may find yourself someday in the middle of a program attempting a rhyme that is, frankly, failing miserably. Never fear. The solution to this pitfall is to jettison the miserable failure and fall back on a known hit. Now is the time to use one of those extra three to five rhymes. If you've never done this program before you might not know which rhymes are "known hits," so here are some suggestions. For Prewalkers, you can never go wrong with "Oh Baby," a cuddly lap song that's sung to the well-known tune of "Playmate," or "Trot, Trot to Boston," a kind of whole-body experience for baby as she or he is jostled and jollied on the knees. Walkers love "Open, Shut Them," a finger game they all seem to know, and "The Wheels on the Bus," a hand game popularized by many early-childhood performers.

Yet, don't dismiss that temporarily stalled rhyme forever. As good as the rhymes presented in this book are, they won't please all of the babies all of the time. The rhyme that was a disaster one day may work for another group, another day, so if you really liked it, give it a second chance.

The rhymes and their directions have been presented in a format to help you as you plunge bravely into this kind of programming. Each of them can be easily photocopied so the copy can then be cut and pasted onto an index card. Used with this book, the cards will be among your most valuable tools. You'll flip through them when deciding what rhymes to do, you'll get used to handling them as you practice the rhymes, and you will have them with you during the program to prompt you with the words. Having the rhymes on individual index cards gives you the flexibility during the actual program to substitute rhymes when needed, the convenience of a place to make notes on the use of a particular rhyme, and the ease to take your program virtually anywhere.

Write the word "Prewalker" or "Walker" in capital letters on the top of each card. If you've selected one of the rhymes that work with both groups, make two copies and two separate cards; this will save you time and energy in searching through a stack of cards for a particular rhyme you've used in one group and now want to use with the other. You will notice that the rhymes indicated as appropriate for both groups sometimes have different directions for Prewalkers than for Walkers. Having two separate cards for each group on which you underline or highlight the appropriate action will eliminate confusion.

As you're going through the rhymes and considering which ones to use, you may remember a favorite childhood verse not included in this collection. If you do remember a rhyme from your childhood, then its rhythm, tone, and language all gave it the child-appeal that made it stick in your memory. Yet beyond these considerations, remember that the rhymes in this book all have an additional element—group-appeal—which enable them to be used successfully in the context of a Mother Goose Time program. So when introducing a personal childhood favorite, or any other untried rhyme, remember to buffer them with well-known, proven crowd pleasers.

Just as this book includes a well-stocked selection of rhymes from which to choose, you will also find an annotated bibliography of charming picture books which work well in this program. These books share common elements, such as bold graphics, bright and pleasing colors, repetitive or rhyming words, simple plots or brief text, and a relatively large page size. Look the titles over. As when choosing the rhymes, it's a good idea to start with ones you already know, but don't hesitate to try out some of the less familiar titles. Read some of the books aloud several times, experimenting with your tone, expression, and speed, until you've discovered those that appeal to you. Have at least two favorites ready to practice for your program because, depending upon the group, you may have time to do two picture books.

Board books are traditionally the first choice for infants—one- or two-word text accompanying each simple picture—on sturdy, stiff pages that stand up to a child's eager grasp. However, these same considerations do not go into selecting a book for group use, since the babies at Mother Goose Time do not usually get their hands on the book. Also, the limited text of most board books generally requires embellishment and interactive interpretation between the reading adult and the listening child that is outside the scope and aims of a Mother Goose Time program.

Beyond board books, there are many highly suitable books from which to choose for use in Mother Goose Time. Aside from the characteristics mentioned above—simple repetitive text, bold graphics, and large page size—keep in mind that many books that prove successful in Mother Goose Time are usually thought of as "lap" books. Quiet, soothing stories that a parent might choose to read at bedtime can also work in the Mother Goose Time group because of the gentle, intimate atmosphere that this program nurtures. A perfect example of this type of book is *Where Does the Brown Bear Go?* by Nicki Weiss (Greenwillow, 1989). The rhythm and cadence of this simple verse soothes young listeners, holding them spellbound. Recognizable animal figures leap, fly, and walk across each page, leading the child along with them. The homey touch of calling the listener "Honey" establishes familiarity and brings the child immediately into the story. The final illustration shows the child asleep in his bed, surrounded by the stuffed animals featured in the book. And the last line "And everyone is home" is a subtle segue for closing the Mother Goose Time program because it mentions home, just the place where the "goslings," as we call the babies in our group, will probably be headed after the program.

A book is a great attention-getter. Although you might want to use it earlier in your program, we have found that reading the book toward the end gives the program closure and acts as a final reminder that Mother Goose Time is indeed literature-based. By that time in your program, you have used the rhymes to establish a rapport and an intimacy with the babies, and by then, they will trust you enough to allow you to read the book to them.

Advertisement

Now that you've done so much work planning your program, you want to make sure that you have babies attend. Go beyond the usual methods you use for advertising library programs, such as newspaper announcements or posters. Flyers can be sent to places where you're going to reach parents and caregivers of young children—the local pediatricians' offices, day-care centers, Mom-and-Tot drop-in centers, toy stores, bookstores, juvenile shoe and clothing stores, lobbies of housing developments, and birthing centers and hospitals. Reciprocate with other agencies in your town, such as the recreation department and school board, to advertise each other's programs. Save money and paper by grouping all of your preschool programs on one flyer. This can breathe new life into programs that may have been in place for some time in addition to highlighting your brand-new Mother Goose Time program. Create a bookmark, listing on one side the upcoming dates for your Mother Goose Time programs for the current programming season and, on the other side, some suggested titles of Mother Goose collections and books for babies.

Word-of-mouth is also a great (and inexpensive!) advertising technique. Parents who have attended your program will tell other people about it. But you should also spread the word. Greet new parents in your library and invite them to bring their babies to Mother Goose Time. If you live in the community where you work, you will have opportunities outside the library to meet potential goslings and their adults who will be delighted to hear about your program.

Registration

If your advertising has been successful, you will be deluged by adults eager to attend your program. To avoid total chaos, you must limit the size of the group. For every baby who attends, there will also be at least one accompanying adult, maybe siblings, and for each group there will always be several assorted strollers. You must have room for all of them. Ten to fifteen babies is a workable number for any session. That size, although it may seem small, allows you to maintain the kind of contact you need for the program to be effective and enables the program to be as gentle and intimate as it should be.

The following information should be at the top of a clear, understandable registration sheet:

- Name of the program
- Developmental level of children eligible for the program
- Day and time of the program
- Date registration opens
- Maximum number of babies who can register

When indicating the developmental level, i.e. Walker or Pre-walker, remember to set a maximum chronological age for the Walker groups, so you don't end up with children who are too old for the program. If you are taking registration for more than one group on any one day, make sure you have a separate sheet for each group. When registering a child for Mother Goose Time, in addition to the child's full name, be sure to get a telephone number in case the program needs to be changed or canceled. For statistics, you may also want to know the age of the child and whether they are residents of your community.

Since this is a new program, you need to explain Mother Goose Time to your staff so they understand what it is and who can register. Attach a brief explanatory paragraph to the top of the registration sheet as a reminder to those who will be talking to the public about the program. An important detail which staff should always

point out when explaining Mother Goose Time to the public is that
its participants sit on the floor. This will allow people with any physical limitations to make any necessary arrangements that will be
helpful to them.

Take registration in advance of the program. You may already
have an established lead time for registration of other programs; if
so, use that. If not, two weeks should be sufficient, especially if you
do this program on a monthly basis. We caution you not to accept
registration for the next session immediately following the current
one or you may never broaden the scope of people you want to reach,
because you will end up programming to the same ten to fifteen
babies and their caregivers every month. The same thing is likely to
happen if you try to conduct this program as a series. As a single
monthly event, this program will provide as many different people as
possible with an opportunity to attend.

Even if you make it a practice to take waiting lists for other
preregistered programs, you may find them unworkable for this kind
of program. Because you are programming to babies and their caregivers, cancellations will usually be at the last minute, preventing

you from calling people on the waiting list. By the same token, it's unrealistic to expect people on a waiting list to drop everything to come to Mother Goose Time on a moment's notice. One solution we have discovered works nicely is to allow "walk-ins." We have adopted an unspoken practice to let unregistered babies and caregivers join a program when there are openings caused by last-minute cancellations or no-shows.

Rehearsal

More than merely rehearsal, the process described here is one of becoming comfortable with every aspect of your new, untried program. There are five parts of Mother Goose Time you should become accustomed to: the rhymes, the order in which you plan to use them, the cards your rhymes are printed on, the book you'll be reading, and the room or space you'll be using.

Though when initially selecting the rhymes, you tried them out and discovered those that were right for you, now it is necessary to really get to know them, in much the same way a storyteller gets to know a story. The rhymes should almost become a part of you. The obvious and most convenient method involves saying the rhymes aloud repeatedly, practicing and experimenting with your pacing and tone. But, just as in practice for storytelling, you'll soon need to try them out on people.

One way is to try out some rhymes on the babies who come into your library. Such a practice method, however, may not suit your personality, so don't feel you have to do it, but perhaps you'll feel enough at ease with a patron to tap their baby's bare foot and say, "Shoe the old horse, shoe the old mare/But let the little pony run bare, bare, bare." It's a great icebreaker and can be a natural part of a conversation about the Mother Goose Time program. Most babies will love having a rhyme said to them individually this way; their parents will be flattered by the attention paid to their child; and you will have snuck in some painless practice.

Once you become comfortable with the rhymes individually, run through them in the order you hope to use them, so you get a feeling for how the program will flow. Just as a rhyme has a rhythm, your program will have a rhythm, too. The order in which you do the rhymes determines that rhythm. But, generally, it is best to work the group up slowly in activity level, letting it peak roughly at the middle of your session and bringing the activity level back down a bit in anticipation of reading a story toward the latter part. After the book, a final quiet-time rhyme or lullaby can be used as a transition to the program's end.

So, try doing a couple of lap rhymes after your "Hello Song," then try some imitation rhymes, followed by two or three activity rhymes. You can start reducing the activity level with a couple more imitation rhymes, and by that time you'll be ready to read the book. Once again, you should not be married to your prearranged order in case one of the rhymes proves less than successful and you find yourself needing a substitute. Luckily, you will have a few on hand, ready for use.

Although flexibility is the key to a successful, rewarding Mother Goose Time, the program will still need some structure to help it work well. This can be as simple as maintaining the same opening and closing rhyme in each program, always including several familiar, dependable rhymes, and using a good mix of activity levels in the rhymes similar to the one described above. Flexibility will allow you to respond to the energy and rhythm of the group as the program progresses, jettisoning those "miserable failures" mentioned earlier, with the confidence that whatever structure you had established has not totally deteriorated.

Another aspect to rehearsal involves practicing the use of your rhyme cards. As you become comfortable handling them, you will discover another benefit to having the rhymes on index cards: it's so easy to flip through from one rhyme to another. The cards are essential to both the flexibility and structure of your program. No matter what rhyme you need, you will never be unable to find it. You won't look like you are searching through pages of a script for a particular rhyme; instead, you can just flip through the cards until you find the rhyme you want.

Once you have all these things well in hand, practice the book you'll be using until you feel comfortable with it. Read it aloud several times until you almost know it by heart. Reading to a group of babies—especially when some of them might be crawling into your lap to snuggle up close or point to familiar objects—is very different from reading stories to the usual preschool crowd who already know what to do in story hour.

If possible, practice the rhymes and book in the programming area you'll be using, so you can be as comfortable as possible during the actual program. This will also give you an opportunity to see any problems that might crop up with the space, e.g. exposed electrical outlets that should be covered, tables or chairs that should be removed, toys or other display items that could prove distracting. Removing, covering, or stabilizing all potential problems ahead of time will save you untold aggravation.

You should also decide where and how your babies and their caregivers will arrange themselves for the program. If you have carpet squares, you can use them to create a circle before the people enter the area. If not, it will be up to you to urge them into a circle as they come in and are deciding where to sit. They may walk in expecting chairs to be set up and will look to you for direction; so be quick on the draw in telling them how to arrange themselves. Make it easy on yourself—and the adults and babies—by indicating the circle in some fashion, perhaps by marking the floor with masking or cloth book tape. Carpet squares do work best, so if you don't have them, we urge you to try to get them. It may be possible, with a little persuasion, to obtain a donation, as we did, from a local carpet dealer. Or, if your budget allows, go to a preschool supply house and buy storytime mats.

Decide ahead of time if there will be sufficient room for strollers. If space is at a premium in your programming area, find a safe, convenient location for the strollers to be left while their owners are in Mother Goose Time. Though most public buildings today are accessible for strollers, emergencies may arise, such as elevators that are out of service, that prevent the participants from getting to you on time. You may need to plan alternate ways of getting the adults and babies to your program.

It's a good idea to display Mother Goose rhyme collections, or other appropriate picture books, for adults to take home with them after the program. But be sure the display does not become another source of distraction during the program. Arrange the books in an area separate from the program yet visible and accessible enough to catch their attention. You'll find a list of some titles that we've displayed with good results on page 123.

Program

Greeting

You've planned it and you've practiced it and you're prepared. Now it's here: Your first Mother Goose Time program. Although the time sharing the rhymes and songs only lasts for about twenty minutes, the time you spend with the participants before (and after) that, are

integral parts of the program, as well. Since this is a sharing program, don't hide in the story room until "show time." Come out into the library, meet the babies and check off the registration sheet to see who's arrived. Make sure everyone feels comfortable and welcome. Greeting the caregiver and complimenting a baby's outfit requires minimal effort but yields maximum results. Build an initial rapport with the babies and their adults, and the atmosphere of the program will be enhanced by it. The caregivers will feel good about the program even before they've gone in and, sensing this, their babies will react accordingly.

As you go around with your clipboard, checking off the names of those who have preregistered, you will undoubtedly encounter some people who are not on the list. Whether good luck brought them into the library at just the right time or they have decided to accompany a registered participant, you need to make a quick decision on how to handle these drop-ins. Chances are there will be room to accommodate them since there are usually some cancellations and no-shows. You need to make them aware, however, that they will be joining the group on a standby basis and urge them to preregister in the future.

You may be inclined to use a stuffed Mother Goose or other figure as an icebreaker to help you greet the babies. Although stuffed animals and other realia play an important role in many libraries, we have found that babies can be intimidated or even frightened by an unfamiliar toy, especially when it's being held by somebody they don't know. So don't think you need to rely on any prop. Your lilting tone and cheerful expression will be sufficient enticement to lure any baby into a Mother Goose Time program. If you do decide to use a stuffed animal as an introductory prop, and carry it with you into the programming area, remember it's a potential source of distraction and have a handy place to stow it.

Speaking of distractions, remember that very young children rarely travel without that special "lovey" or a bottle. While you cannot, and should not, prevent these items from coming with their owners into Mother Goose Time, you should try to keep unnecessary books and realia out of the programming area and from becoming a source of argument between some goslings, thereby diverting the group's attention.

Transition to Programming Area

You're probably going to be programming in an area separate from where you have been greeting everyone. The distance you travel is unimportant—your programming area may be as close as the other side of a bookcase; or you may need to go to an entirely different room. Whatever the distance, you need to make a transition from the general library space to the programming area. Announcing, "It's Mother Goose Time!" with a cheerful, forceful voice is our signal that the transition to the program has begun. We repeat this announcement as we move toward the programming room, inviting the babies to: "Come along, and bring your grown-ups."

At the door to the room, we tell them, "Pull up a carpet square," and then one of us reenters the library itself to check for stragglers. Though you should make a reasonable effort to get all your participants into the programming area, do not attempt to force reluctant babies to join the group. Tell the child's adult that if the child decides that she or he wants to come in, they can always do so later.

You might prefer to marshal everyone into a group and proceed to your area in a line. The familiar words to "Down by the Station" were used at one time in this library to herald the start of Mother Goose Time. Imagine fifteen babies in strollers, assorted adults, and siblings and you really get a picture of "puffer-bellies all in a row"!

Whatever you've done to get all the participants into the programming area, once they are there, you want them to arrange themselves into a circle on the floor. If you have already indicated a circle in some fashion, so much the better. If not, gently steer them into a circle and get them settled so that the program can start. Don't forget to leave a space for yourself, and make sure you have your cards and book.

Leading the Program

After you've joined the circle (and you may want to sit on the book to keep it away from curious little hands), the first thing you should do is introduce yourself. It's important to start with a formal "Hello, my name is . . . " kind of introduction, even if you think most people know who you are. This establishes a friendly welcoming tone, making it easier for everyone else to introduce themselves, too.

Before inviting the adults to tell you their names, say something about the program and set out the ground rules (few though they are). The following is an example of the type of introduction we use:

Welcome to Mother Goose Time. This is a language-enrichment program in which we do rhymes and songs and finger plays. The main thing is to have fun, so if your child is unhappy or uncomfortable, please take him or her outside until he or she calms down. We won't be insulted; we all know we are working with little ones and sometimes they change their minds about being here. Also, don't worry if your child roams a bit during the program. We try to be as flexible as you are, and we know the babies are taking it in, even if they are not sitting on your lap, watching us.

However you end up saying it, the three main points in your opening statement should be: it's a language-enrichment program; if the baby is crying, remove him or her from the group; and don't force the child to stay seated by your side.

Invite the adults to introduce themselves and the babies they've brought with them. By the time you have gone around the circle, everyone in the area should have a name, including siblings and grandparents. There are no strangers in Mother Goose Time.

Now is the time to use that opening song you have chosen and practiced. In our program, after the last adult has made his or her introduction, we say, "And now let's start Mother Goose the way we always do, by singing our Hello Song." As you go along, you need to present each song and rhyme as if no one in the group has ever heard it before. Sing it slowly and clearly but enthusiastically. Do the motions as distinctly as possible, even if it requires that you pretend to have a baby bouncing on your knees. Sometimes, you may need a brief introductory statement (the key word is "brief") to prepare the adults for a particular rhyme. For example, when we do our "Exercises" chant, we explain that the babies, if they're Walkers, can stand up or remain seated to do this chant, raising their arms as we all say, "Exercises, exercises, let's all do our exercises."

Do each rhyme or song at least twice. Applaud vigorously, adding "hurrays" as needed, between each repetition. You'll find that "giving yourselves a hand" can be the most popular activity in Mother Goose Time. It can also be a great energy charge and morale booster for you.

The only time you don't need to repeat a rhyme is when you've had absolutely no response from the group. The lack of response tells you that you've probably just hit one of those miserable failures. Applaud yourself nonetheless, because the applause itself is such a crowd pleaser. But find something else to move onto, whether it's a substitute you are inserting or simply the next rhyme in your lineup.

Sometimes the group's energy or focus moves away from the program. It's hard to put your finger on why, but you'll know when it's happening. Possibly a cantankerous child has stolen the group's attention, or too many unfamiliar rhymes have been introduced, and you really feel you need to recharge the group. So shuffle your cards and pull out a winner, like "Baby A-Go Go" for Prewalkers or "Head, Shoulders, Knees and Toes" for Walkers—something you know works every time.

Discovering how many rhymes will be enough to fill up a program will be a matter of some trial and error, as you learn not only the number but the pace with which you are comfortable. We usually do anywhere from ten to twelve rhymes in addition to reading a book to the group. So, try that as a guide and add or drop a few as you feel the need.

The end of the program is the best time to read a simple picture book. Reading a book to a group of babies differs dramatically from reading aloud in a preschool story hour. Babies are an amorphous group and, as such, tend to control you rather than the other way around. Many a time we have had to hold the book above our heads as one or more eager babies have crawled into our laps, trying to experience the book up close. And, even if they don't feel compelled to examine the book, many babies are "lap-listeners." They have a Pavlovian response to an open book: they back their bottoms into the lap of the adult reading the book!

Remember to always select and practice two books for each program. This will give you last-minute flexibility in deciding which one to read, as well as a second book in case the response from the group warrants it. Remember to hide the books until you are ready to read them. Sitting on them or tucking them under your carpet square are probably the only measures you can take to keep the books from inquisitive little hands.

If, despite careful selection and practice, the book doesn't go over well, try to keep a good attitude and a sense of humor. Sharing the book shouldn't be an effort for you or the babies; so if it isn't working, stop reading it. "The End" is a painless, logical solution, and children usually know what it means. Any adults who realize the book wasn't finished, will also realize it wasn't working and will appreciate your efforts to cut your losses.

The best thing to do after the book, whether it has worked well or not, is to sing a lullaby. If the book has succeeded, you can capitalize on the quiet it generated, and extend it by singing a lullaby. On the other hand, singing a soothing, familiar lullaby after a book that was less than successful will draw the babies back to you. Three classic, tender songs that fill the lullaby bill are "Twinkle, Twinkle Little Star," "Rock A Bye Baby," and "Lavender's Blue."

Now that you have nourished the babies with nursery rhymes and sated them with a song, it's time to finish the feast. You don't want to overfeed your babies, so even if the program has gone smoothly, know when to stop—and that is when they are still entranced by the program, not when the babies are begging to leave.

Closing

While the group is still relatively quiet and focused, thank everyone for coming to the program and tell the adults when the next scheduled Mother Goose Time will take place. As long as you keep announcements brief and specific to the Mother Goose Time program, the adults will still leave with the rhymes they have heard singing in their heads and hearts.

Follow the announcements by singing the song you've chosen as your good-bye signature. Children who attend on a regular basis will come to recognize the good-bye song as the signal that Mother Goose Time is over. And just in case they don't, announce to the group: "Now let's end Mother Goose Time the way we always do—by singing our good-bye song." No matter how eventful or tumultuous your program may have been, you can be confident that the good-bye song will be successful and provide closure. This is the only song you have to do just once. But don't forget to applaud enthusiastically after finishing and wave good-bye to the group. Just as clapping is popular, waving good-bye is also a favorite activity with goslings.

Yet another favorite activity for goslings who are Walkers is "helping." A ritual has evolved in our program in which the children "help" us put the carpet squares into a cabinet in our activities room. Even if you plan to leave the carpet squares in a pile in the programming area, be sure to have the children help. They can pick up the square they've been sitting on—and generally the one next to it as well—and carry or drag it over to you, rushing back to the circle for more. Besides having your carpet squares gathered for you, this ritual also gives you the opportunity to thank each child individually for coming, making them feel special and appreciated.

Just as the program really began before you entered the program-

ming area, it continues after the group has left the room. Many of the adults will linger afterward in the library, looking for books and talking to the other parents and caregivers. Be available to suggest some books they might enjoy if those in your display of Mother Goose collections and pictures books are depleted.

When discussing the program with an adult, it can be fun to repeat one of your favorite rhymes for their baby, if he or she looks alert and eager at the sound of your voice. This extends the good feeling of the program and reinforces the intimate nature of Mother Goose Time. Your personal attention will be a small detail of great importance to the adults who brought their babies to your program. They will remember it and bring the babies back again.

Contingencies

Although you will usually have a roomful of eager babies and enthusiastic caregivers responding and sharing with you as you sing, recite, and clap hands, there will be times when all may not go according to plan. Without discouraging you from programming to very young children, we do want to present a realistic picture of what such programming can sometimes entail. There may be babies who are crying for no discernible reason, stragglers who struggle through the door laden with diaper bags and reluctant children just as you announce your "good-bye song," babies who want to leave long before their adults do, the baby who has managed to find the one thing in the entire room that you failed to secure before the program started and is now playing with it, the overly social baby who wants to share the bottle (or dolly or Cheerios or grown-up's lap) belonging to the child next to him, and the overly enthusiastic sibling who tries to teach her six-month-old brother how to clap, even if he doesn't want to learn.

Humorous though these examples might be, they can be overwhelming if you face them during an actual program. While we cannot provide you with a diagram to follow in dealing with difficulties, we want you to remember that when working with children, there are some things that will be beyond your control. But if you have planned your program carefully, and are thoroughly practiced, you will be prepared to meet any challenge. Maintain your sense of humor and flexibility and the problem won't be so overwhelming. Remember that the worst thing that could possibly happen is that you might need to cut your program short, jump right to your good-bye song, and with your brightest smile invite everyone back the following month.

We thought our Mother Goose Time careers were ended once when total bedlam erupted during the picture-book portion of our program. No one was listening, babies were heading for the door like lemmings to a cliff, and even the adults had given up and begun to make lunch plans. What saved us was humor. We looked at each other and burst into laughter. Our hilarity startled the children, freezing them in their tracks, and it released the parents to laugh along with us at our lack of control over their babies. When the laughter died down, we cut our losses, jumped to our good-bye routine and valiantly announced the dates of the next Mother Goose Time program. Contrary to our worst fears, many of the same parents returned the next month, and we are happy to say that the next month's programs ran with nary a hitch.

Evaluation

From the moment the program ends, you will start an informal self-evaluation. How did the program go? Did you like the rhymes that you did? Was the response from both babies and adults what you had hoped? What difficulties arose and how did you deal with them? Did you have enough material? As you begin to answer these questions, you will be setting the groundwork for the next month's program.

But you can't do an honest evaluation of the program without also asking for the public's response. This can be done simply and informally by talking to the adults afterward to elicit their immediate reactions. If you want more extensive reviews, however, you can hand out evaluation forms similar to the one we've provided on page 105. Although it is gratifying to receive positive feedback about the Mother Goose Time you have done, it's not enough to just thank the adults for compliments and feel flattered; nor should you take criticism personally. Use the information you have received, think about what they are saying, and act upon it. Go beyond the specific aspect of the program they liked or disliked and try to determine why they responded as they did. For instance, if you can identify in your own mind why a certain rhyme works, then you can find similar rhymes to introduce into your program with greater confidence. You may also elicit comments about things other than what you have put into the program, such as one parent's comment about another parent's or baby's behavior. This, too, is a valid issue for you to review or consider when thinking about your program and how you conduct it. You may need to revise your opening statement, for example, to be more explicit in your expectations about appropriate behavior.

After the parents have gone, but not too long after the program has ended, you should sit down with your cards and run through the rhymes you've just used. At the least, note the date you used the rhyme on the back of the card. You may want to reshuffle your cards, while the program is fresh in your mind, into an order that you think might work better for you the next time. A more extensive analysis would involve making some comments about the rhyme on the back of the card. You may have discovered that a different motion worked better with the rhyme, or one of the adults in the group may have had an alternate wording or verse that you want to remember. Don't rely upon memory to carry you through until the next time you use the rhyme; instead, note the observation about the rhyme while it's fresh in your mind.

One Final Thought

By now, you have started on the road to successful Mother Goose Time programming. We applaud your energy, enthusiasm, and enterprise. We know these qualities will serve you well, but, if along the programming road ahead, should the way become unclear or the path cluttered, remember this book is here to guide you. Don't fret if your program is not an exact replica of ours. After all, it's not the letter of the program that's important, it's the spirit. Recognize that by entering the world of Mother Goose Time programming, you've accepted our invitation to introduce babies and their adults to the enduring and endearing rhymes and songs that are at the heart of this world.

PART II
RHYMES AND SONGS

Types of Rhymes and Songs

The following rhymes and songs are presented in three categories: *Lap, Imitation,* and *Activity.* Within each category, a (W) for Walker indicates a rhyme suitable for a walking baby, a (P) for Prewalker indicates a rhyme that is best for a baby not yet walking, and a (B) for Both indicates that you can use it with either group. The symbol ♪ indicates a song. Some of the songs have musical notations in the Music Appendix; these are designated by the phrase "(Melody provided)." If the tune is fairly universal, musical notation has not been provided and the term "(Melody traditional)" accompanies the song.

Lap

A Lap rhyme has almost no accompanying physical activity other than rhythmic bouncing. Many of the more traditional Mother Goose rhymes fall into this category.

PIG-A-WIG (P)

This little pig had a rub-a-dub,
This little pig had a scrub-a-
    scrub.
This little pig-a-wig ran upstairs,
This little pig-a-wig called out,
    "Bears."
Down came the jar with a loud
    slam,
And this little pig had all the jam.

Touch one of baby's fingers
    or toes as you say each
    line.

SAT A LITTLE HARE (P)

Round about, round about,
Sat a little hare.
The puppies came and chased
    him,
Right up there!

Circle baby's palm with
    finger.

Walk fingers up arm.
Tickle under arm or chin.

CATCH A WEE MOUSE (P)

Round about, round about,
Catch a wee mouse.
Up a bit, up a bit,
In a wee house.

Circle baby's palm with
    finger.
Walk fingers up arm.
Tickle under arm or chin.

SHOE THE OLD HORSE (P)

Shoe the old horse,
Shoe the old mare,
But let the little pony
Run bare, bare, bare.

Tap soles of feet.

Tap feet together.

JACK BE NIMBLE (P)

Jack be nimble,   Bounce baby on knees.
Jack be quick,
Jack jump over   Lift baby up.
The candlestick.

TOMMY O'FLYNN (P) ♪
(*Melody:* "Mulberry Bush"—*traditional*)

Tommy O'Flynn and his old gray   Bounce baby on knees.
   mare
Went off to see the country fair.
The bridge fell down,   Lower baby between knees.
And the bridge fell in,
And that was the end of Tommy   Bounce rapidly.
   O'Flynn.

RICKETY, RICKETY ROCKING HORSE (P)

Rickety, rickety rocking horse,   Bounce baby on knees in
Over the hills we go.   rhythm.
Rickety, rickety rocking horse,
Giddy-up, giddy-up, whoa!

FLYING MAN (P)

Flying man, flying man,   Bounce baby on knees.
Up in the sky,   Lift baby up.
Where are you going to,   Bounce baby on knees.
Flying so high?   Lift baby up.

Over the mountains,   Bounce baby on knees.
And over the sea,   Lift baby up.
Flying man, flying man,   Bounce baby on knees.
Can't you take me?   Hug baby.

BABY A-GO GO (P) ♪
(Melody provided on page 107)

Baby a-go go,	Bounce on knees.
Hey-ah!	Sway to one side.
Baby a-go go,	Bounce on knees.
Hey-ah!	Sway to other side.
Baby a go-	Bounce on knees.
Oh!	Lift baby up.
Baby a-go go go!	Bounce on knees.

LEG OVER LEG (P)

Leg over leg,	Bounce baby rhythmically on
As the dog went to Dover.	knees.
When he came to a stile,	
Jump—he went over.	Lift baby up on "jump".

RIGADOON (P)

A trot, and a canter,	Bounce baby rhythmically on
A gallop and over.	knees.
Out of the saddle,	
And roll in the clover.	
Rigadoon, rigadoon,	
Now let him fly.	
Sit him on father's foot,	
Jump him up high.	Lift baby up on last line.

THESE ARE BABY'S FINGERS (P)

These are baby's fingers,	Kiss or touch fingers/toes.
These are baby's toes,	
This is baby's belly button,	Touch belly.
Round and round it goes.	Circle belly button.

MOTHER AND FATHER AND UNCLE JOHN (P)

Mother and Father and Uncle
   John
Went to town one by one.

Mother fell off,
Father fell off,
But Uncle John went on and on
   and on.

Bounce on knees.

Dip to one side.
Dip to other side.
Bounce on knees.

ROUND AND ROUND THE GARDEN (B)

Round and round the garden,
Goes the teddy bear.
One step, two step,
Tickle 'em under there.

Circle belly with finger.

Walk fingers up chest.
Tickle under chin.

OH, BABY (B) ♪
(*Melody provided on page 118*)

Say, say oh, baby,
Come here and clap with me,
And bring your happy smile,
Bounce on my lap so free.
Shake shake your hands now,
Shake shake your bottom too,
And shake your tootsies ten,
Let's do it again!

Bounce baby on lap and
   move hands or feet where
   indicated.

RIDE A COCK HORSE (P) ♪
(*Melody provided on page 120*)

Ride a cock horse
To Banbury Cross,
To see a fine lady
Upon a white horse.

Bounce baby rhythmically on
   lap.

With rings on her fingers,   Touch baby's fingers.
And bells on her toes,   Touch baby's toes.
She shall have music,
Wherever she goes.

WHAT ARE YOU WEARING? (B) ♪
(*Melody:* "Mary had a Little Lamb"—*traditional*)

(Name) has a (color) shirt on.
(Color) shirt on, (color) shirt on.
(Name) has a (color) shirt on.
I see him (her) here today.

Insert child's name and color of shirt as appropriate

TOUCH YOUR NOSE (B) ♪
(*Melody:* "Mulberry Bush"—*traditional*)

Touch your nose, touch your chin,   Touch parts of baby as
That's the way this game begins.   indicated.
Touch your eyes, touch your
     knees,
Now pretend you feel a breeze.   Blow gently on baby's face.

Touch your hair, touch one ear,
Touch your two red lips right
     here.
Touch your elbows where they
     bend,
That's the way this touch game
     ends.

This could be done as an imitation rhyme for the older babies, who will probably not tolerate your touching their faces and will want to do it themselves.

TROT, TROT TO BOSTON (P)

Trot, trot to Boston,	Bounce baby on knee.
Trot, trot to Lynn.	
Look out Baby,	Lower baby gently through
You're going to fall in!	legs on "in."

VALENTINES (B) ♪
(*Melody:* "Ride a Cock Horse"—*provided on page 120*)

Valentines, valentines,	
Valentines true.	
I'll find a nice one,	
and give it to you.	Touch or tickle baby.
Flowers are sweet,	
This is true.	
But, for my valentine,	Point to self.
I'll choose you!	Point to baby.

IF YOUR FINGERS (B)

If your fingers wiggle,	Wiggle fingers and interlace
Cross them one by one,	them until folded tightly.
Until they hug each other.	
It really is quite fun.	

THIS LITTLE PIG (B)

This little pig went to market,	Touch baby's fingers or toes.
This little pig stayed home,	
This little pig had roast beef,	
This little pig had none,	
And this little pig cried,	
"Wee, wee, wee,	Walk fingers up child's arm
I can't find my way home."	or leg.

RAIN ON THE ROOFTOPS (B)

Rain on the rooftops,
Rain on the tree,
Rain on the green grass,
But not on me.

Pretend to point to each
  object.

Point to self and shake head
  "no."

RAIN, RAIN GO AWAY (B) ♪
(*Melody provided on page 120*)

Rain, rain go away,
Come again some other day.
All these children want to play.

Rain, rain go away,
We've seen you enough today.
Now it's time for us to play.

PAT A CAKE (B)

Pat a cake, pat a cake,
Baker's man.
Bake me a cake,
As fast as you can.

Clap hands rhythmically.

Roll it, and pat it,
And mark it with a B.
And put it in the oven
For Baby and me.

Roll and clap hands.
Trace "B" on palm.
Extend both hands.
Point to baby and self.

HERE IS A DOUGHNUT (B)

Here is a doughnut,
Round and fat.
There's a hole
In the middle,
But you can't eat that.

Extend fist.

Show circle of finger and
  thumb.
Shake head "no."

JACK-O-LANTERN (B)

Carve a jack-o-lantern,
On Halloween night.
He has a big mouth,   Point to mouth.
But he doesn't bite.
He has two big eyes,   Point to eyes.
But he cannot see.
He's a funny jack-o-lantern,
As happy as can be.

JACK-O-LANTERN II (B)

A face so round,   Hands in circle.
And eyes so bright.   Touch eyes.
A nose that glows,   Touch nose.
My, what a sight!
A fiery mouth,   Touch mouth.
With jolly grin.   Grin.
No arms, no legs,   Shake arms, legs.
Just head to chin.   One hand on head and other
                                          on chin.

RUB A DUB DUB (B)

Rub a dub dub,   Rub baby on belly in a
Three men in a tub.   circular motion.
And who do you think they be?
The butcher, the baker,   Tap belly three times.
The candlestick maker.
Throw them out—   Jerk thumb over shoulder or
Knaves, all three.   tickle baby.

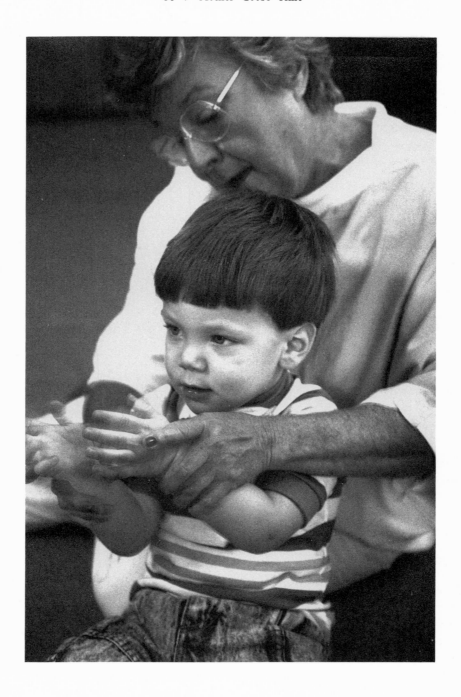

CLAP HANDS (B) ♪
(Melody provided on page 108)

Clap hands, clap hands,
Till Daddy comes home.
Clap hands, clap hands,
Till Mommy comes home.

Clap your hands with baby
or sit baby on knee facing
you and clap baby's hands
for him or her.

ROUND BALL (P)

Round ball, round ball,
Pull your tinky hair.
One slice, two slice,

Tickle under there.

Circle finger on baby's palm.
Gently tug on baby's hair.
Run pointer finger along
baby's arm.
Tickle on belly or under arm.

TICKLE ON KNEE (P)

If you are a lady (gentleman),
As I suppose you'll be,
You'll neither laugh nor smile,
As I tickle you on your knee.

Trace your finger around
child's knee in circular
motion.

BIG A (P)

Big A,
Little a,
Bouncing B.
The cat's in the cupboard,
And he can't see!
Peek-a-boo!
I see you!

Open baby's arms.
Bring baby's hands together.
Bounce baby on knee.

Cover baby's eyes.
Take hands away.

MARY HAD A LITTLE LAMB—EXERCISE (P) ♪
(*Melody traditional*)

Mary had a little lamb,
Little lamb, little lamb.
Mary had a little lamb,
Whose fleece was white as snow.

Hand to knee and stretch out,
Stretch out, stretch out.
Hand to knee and stretch out,
It's fun to play with you.

Stretch baby's hand from
knee to over head and back
again.

FIVE LITTLE FINGERS (P)

Five little fingers on this hand,
Five little fingers on that.
A dear little nose,
A mouth like a rose.
Two little cheeks so tiny and fat,
Two eyes, two ears,
And ten little toes.
We'll watch baby every day,
And see how she (he) grows.

Point to parts of baby as
rhyme indicates.

ONE POTATO (P)

Legs apart,
Legs together,
Legs apart,
BOO!
Legs apart,
Legs together,
I Love You!

With baby lying on back
facing you, gently open and
close baby's legs as
indicated.

One potato,
Two potato,
Three potato,
BOO!

Cross baby's legs one over
the other on each count.

Four potato,
Five potato,
I Love You!

Legs apart,
Legs together,
Legs apart,
BOO!
Legs apart,
Legs together,
I Love You!

With baby lying on back facing you, gently open and close baby's legs as indicated.

YANKEE DOODLE—EXERCISE (P) ♪
(*Melody traditional*)

Arms up high above the head,
Arms down low beside you.
Arms up high above the head,
Smile and brush noses.

Yankee Doodle keep it up,
Yankee Doodle Dandy.
Arms up high above the head,
Smile and brush noses.

Gently raise and lower baby's arms as indicated.

Touch baby's nose.

Raise baby's arms.
Touch baby's nose.

RIDING GAME (B)

This is the way the farmer rides,
A-jiggety-jog, a-jiggety-jog.

This is the way the lady rides,
A-prance, a-prance.

This is the way the gentleman rides,
A-gallop, a-gallop, a-gallop.

Rock baby side to side on knees.

Raise and lower baby slowly with knees.

Bounce baby quickly up and down on knees.

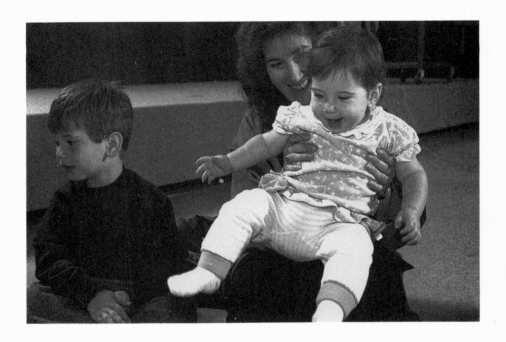

Although this might *seem* appropriate only for the Prewalkers, it is a big success for the Walkers as well. If, during the verse for "the gentleman," you pause before saying "A-gallop" and then do the gallop part as fast as you can, they will love it. As they get to know the rhyme, they will quiver in anticipation waiting for the punch line of "A-gallop" as fast as you can do it.

TO MARKET, TO MARKET (P) ♪
(Melody provided on page 120)

To market, to market, To buy a fat pig. Home again, home again, Jiggety-jig.	Baby on knees; gently bounce up and down.
To market, to market, To buy a fat hog. Home again, home again, Jiggety-jog.	Baby on knees; gently bounce up and down.

CHIN CHOPPER (P)

Knock on the door,
Peep in.
Turn the latch,
Walk in.
Chin chopper, chin chopper, chin.

Tap baby's forehead.
Touch eyebrow.
Tap nose.
Touch lips.
Grasp baby's chin and wiggle
　it up and down.

HERE SITS THE LORD MAYOR (P)

Here sits the Lord Mayor,
Here sit his men.
Here sits the cockadoodle,
Here sits the hen.
Here sit the little chickens,
Here they run in.
Chin chopper, chin chopper,
Chin chopper, chin.

Touch forehead.
Touch eyes.
Touch right cheek.
Touch left cheek.
Touch teeth.
Touch mouth.
Grasp baby's chin and wiggle
　it up and down.

LITTLE SNOWBOY (B)

We make one little snowboy,
And his name is Fred.
We make two little snowboys,
They went riding on a sled.
We make three little snowboys,
And march them off to bed.

Hold up folded paper figures
　to reveal one snowboy.
Unfold to reveal two
　snowboys.
Unfold to reveal three
　snowboys.
"Walk" them away.

This is done with a set of precut snowboys that are unfolded slowly
as you say the rhyme. Photocopy, cut, and fold the pattern on page 56
to make a chain of snowboys.

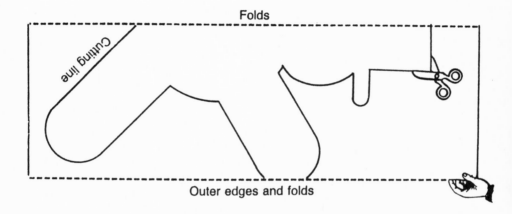

Folds

Cutting line

Outer edges and folds

SIMPLE SIMON (B)

Simple Simon met a pieman,
Going to the fair.
Says Simple Simon to the
    pieman,
Let me taste your ware.
Says the pieman to Simple
    Simon,
Show me first your penny.
Says Simple Simon to the
    pieman,
Indeed I have not any!

Hold up first one thumb,
    then the other.
Nod one thumb at the other.

Nod the second thumb at the
    first.

Nod the first thumb.

Shake head no.

DIDDLE DIDDLE DUMPLING (P)

Diddle, diddle, dumpling, my son
  John,
Went to bed with his trousers on.
One shoe off, and one shoe on,
Diddle, diddle, dumpling, my son
  John.

Bicycle baby's legs.

Pat each foot.
Bicycle baby's legs.

The following three rhymes are fairly traditional and highly portable—transferable to everyday life by their common subject matter.
While none are accompanied by directions, their use is obviated by
their content.

I EAT MY PEAS WITH HONEY (B)

I eat my peas with honey.
I've done it all my life.
It makes the peas taste funny,
But it keeps them on the knife.

One for me and one for you.
If there's one left what will we do?
Take up a knife and cut it in two,
Now one's for me and one's for you.

Though this rhyme describes little action in the context of the program, this is a natural one for the parent to use when the baby is in
the high chair to accompany the "action" of feeding the baby.

STOPLIGHT (B)

Red says stop,
And green says go.
Yellow says wait,
You'd better go slow.

POLLY PUT THE KETTLE ON (B) ♪
(Melody provided on page 119)

Polly put the kettle on.
Polly put the kettle on.
Polly put the kettle on.
We'll all have tea.

Sukey take it off again.
Sukey take it off again.
Sukey take it off again.
They've all gone away.

It's possible to insert any child's name in this song or change the activity you are doing, e.g. "Sally put the spoons away."

PUSSY CAT, PUSSY CAT (B)

Pussy cat, pussy cat,
Where have you been?
I've been to London
To look at the queen.

Pussy cat, pussy cat,
What did you there?
I frightened a little mouse
Under the chair.

OLD KING COLE (B)

Old King Cole was a merry old soul,
And a merry old soul was he.
He called for his pipe,
And he called for his bowl,
And he called for his fiddlers three.

OLD MOTHER GOOSE (P) ♪
(Melody provided on page 118)

Old Mother Goose,
When she wanted to wander,
Would ride through the air,
On a very fine gander.
Old Father Gander,
When the wind was fast and loose,
Would ride through the air,
On a very fine goose.

HEY DIDDLE DIDDLE (P) ♪
(Melody provided on page 112)

Hey diddle, diddle,
The cat and the fiddle,
The cow jumped over the moon.
The little dog laughed
To see such sport,
And the dish ran away with the spoon.

HIGGLETY PIGGLETY POP (P)

Higglety pigglety pop,
The dog has eaten the mop.
The pig's in a hurry,
The cat's in a flurry,
Higglety pigglety pop.

BEES DO NOT LIKE THE SNOW (B)

Bees do not like the snow.
I will tell you why I know.
Once I sat upon a bee,
And he was much too hot for me.

ROOSTER CROWS (P)

One, two, three,
Baby's on my knee.
Rooster crows,
And away he (she) goes.

HICKORY DICKORY DOCK (B) ♪
(Melody provided on page 112)

Hickory, dickory, dock,
The mouse ran up the clock.
The clock struck one,
And down he run,
Hickory, dickory dock.

OLD MACDONALD (B) ♪
(Melody traditional)

Old MacDonald had a farm, e-i-e-i-o.
And on his farm he had a cow, e-i-e-i-o.
With a moo, moo here and a moo, moo there,
Here a moo, there a moo, everywhere a moo, moo.
Old MacDonald had a farm, e-i-e-i-o.

Repeat with other animals and appropriate sounds. Although you
can probably do this with both groups, the older babies will be more
apt to join you in making the animal sounds.

LITTLE MISS MUFFET (B)

Little Miss Muffet
Sat on her tuffet,
Eating her curds and whey.
Along came a spider,
And sat down beside her,
And frightened Miss Muffet away.

BAA, BAA, BLACK SHEEP (B) ♪
(Melody traditional)

Baa, baa, black sheep,
Have you any wool?
Yes, sir, yes, sir,
Three bags full.
One for my master,
And one for my dame,
And one for the little boy,
Who lives down the lane.

PETER, PETER PUMPKIN EATER (B)

Peter, Peter, pumpkin eater,
Had a wife and couldn't keep her.
Put her in a pumpkin shell,
And there he kept her very well.

HOT CROSS BUNS (B) ♪
(Melody provided on page 113)

Hot cross buns,
Hot cross buns,
One a penny, two a penny,
Hot cross buns.
If your daughters do not like them,
Give them to your sons.
One a penny, two a penny,
Hot cross buns.

JACK AND JILL (B) ♪
(Melody traditional)

Jack and Jill went up the hill,
To fetch a pail of water.
Jack fell down and broke his crown,
And Jill came tumbling after.

HUMPTY DUMPTY (B) ♪
(Melody provided on page 113)

Humpty Dumpty sat on a wall.
Humpty Dumpty had a great fall.
All the king's horses,
And all the king's men,
Couldn't put Humpty together again.

IT'S RAINING, IT'S POURING (B) ♪
(Melody traditional)

It's raining, it's pouring.
The old man is snoring.
He went to bed,
And bumped his head,
And didn't get up 'til the morning.

ONE, TWO, BUCKLE MY SHOE (B)

One, two, buckle my shoe.
Three, four, shut the door.
Five, six, pick up sticks.
Seven, eight, lay them straight.
Nine, ten, let's do it again.

SING A SONG OF SIXPENCE (B) ♪
(Melody traditional)

Sing a song of sixpence,
A pocket full of rye.
Four and twenty blackbirds,
Baked in a pie.

When the pie was open,
The birds began to sing.
Wasn't that a tasty treat
To set before the king?

MARY, MARY, QUITE CONTRARY (B)

Mary, Mary, quite contrary,
How does your garden grow?
With silver bells and cockle shells,
And pretty maids all in a row.

LITTLE BOY BLUE (B) ♪
(*Melody provided on page 116*)

Little boy blue,
Come blow your horn.
The sheep's in the meadow,
The cow's in the corn.

But where's the boy
Who looks after the sheep?
He's under the haystack,
Fast asleep.

Will you wake him?
No, not I,
For if I do,
He's sure to cry.

THREE WISE MEN OF GOTHAM (B)

Three wise men of Gotham
Went to sea in a bowl.
And if the bowl had been stronger,
My song had been longer.

LITTLE JACK HORNER (B) ♪
(Melody provided on page 116)

Little Jack Horner
Sat in the corner,
Eating a Christmas pie.
He put in his thumb,
And pulled out a plum,
And said, "What a good boy am I."

JACK SPRAT (B)

Jack Sprat could eat no fat.
His wife could eat no lean.
And so, between them both,
They licked the platter clean.

LITTLE BO PEEP (B)

Little Bo Peep has lost her sheep,
And cannot tell where to find them.
Leave them alone and they'll come home,
And bring their tails behind them.

MARY HAD A LITTLE LAMB (B) ♪
(Melody traditional)

Mary had a little lamb,
Little lamb, little lamb.
Mary had a little lamb,
Whose fleece was white as snow.

He followed her to school one day,
School one day, school one day.
He followed her to school one day,
Which was against the rule.

It made the children laugh and play,
Laugh and play, laugh and play.
It made the children laugh and play,
To see a lamb at school.

HICKETY PICKETY (B)

Hickety, pickety, my black hen,
She lays eggs for gentlemen.
Gentlemen come every day,
To see what my black hen doth lay.
Sometimes nine and sometimes ten,
Hickety, pickety, my black hen.

The following couplets can each be used to introduce the month in which your program takes place. In September, there is a choice, one more gentle than the other.

MONTH RHYMES (B)

JANUARY
January brings the snow,
Makes our feet and fingers glow.

FEBRUARY
February brings the rain,
Thaws the frozen lake again.

MARCH
March brings breezes, loud and shrill,
To stir the dancing daffodil.

APRIL
April brings the primrose sweet,
Scatters daisies at our feet.

MAY
May brings flocks of pretty lambs,
Skipping by their fleecy dams.

JUNE
June brings tulips, lilies, roses,
Fills the children's hands with posies.

JULY
Hot July brings cooling showers,
Apricots and gillyflowers.

AUGUST
August brings the sheaves of corn,
Then the harvest home is borne.

SEPTEMBER
Warm September brings the fruit,
Sportsmen then begin to shoot.

September blows soft,
Till the fruit's in the loft.

OCTOBER
Fresh October brings the pheasant,
Then to gather nuts is pleasant.

NOVEMBER
Dull November brings the blast,
Then the leaves are whirling fast.

DECEMBER
Chill December brings the sleet,
Blazing fire and Christmas treat.

STAR LIGHT, STAR BRIGHT (B)

Star light, star bright,
First star I see tonight.
I wish I may, I wish I might,
Have the wish I wish tonight.

SEE SAW MARGERY DAW (P) ♪
(Melody traditional)

See saw Margery Daw,
Baby will love when we hug her (him).
Baby will have all the hugs in the world,
Because she (he) knows that we love her (him).

LONDON BRIDGE (B) ♪
(Melody traditional)

London bridge is falling down,
Falling down, falling down.
London bridge is falling down,
My fair lady.

With the Prewalkers, this song can simply be sung. With the Walkers, you can have the babies join hands with their adults and swing their arms back and forth as they sing the song.

The following rhymes are all lullabies—perfect for soothing baby both in the library and at home.

TWINKLE, TWINKLE LITTLE STAR (B) ♪
(Melody traditional)

Twinkle, twinkle little star,
How I wonder what you are.
Up above the world so high,
Like a diamond in the sky.
Twinkle, twinkle little star,
How I wonder what you are.

ROCK A BYE BABY (B) ♪
(Melody traditional)

Rock a bye baby,
On the tree top.
When the winds blow,
The cradle will rock.
When the bough breaks,
The cradle will fall.
And down will come baby,
Cradle and all.

LAVENDER'S BLUE (B) ♪
(Melody provided on page 115)

Lavender's blue, dilly dilly,
Lavender's green.
When I am king, dilly dilly,
You shall be queen.

Who told you so, dilly dilly,
Who told you so.
'Twas my own heart, dilly dilly,
That told me so.

Roses are red, dilly dilly,
Violets are blue.
Because you love me, dilly dilly,
I will love you.

ALL THE PRETTY LITTLE HORSES (B) ♪
(Melody provided on page 107)

Hush-a-bye, don't you cry,
Go to sleepy, little baby.
When you wake, you shall have
All the pretty little horses.
Blacks and bays, dapples and grays,
All the pretty little horses.
Hush-a-bye, don't you cry,
Go to sleepy, little baby.

HUSH LITTLE BABY (B) ♪
(Melody traditional)

Hush, little baby, don't say a word,
Papa's going to buy you a mockingbird.
And if that mockingbird don't sing,
Papa's going to buy you a diamond ring.

If that diamond ring turns brass,
Papa's going to buy you a looking glass.
And if that looking glass gets broke,
Papa's going to buy you a billy goat.

And if that billy goat won't pull,
Papa's going to buy you a cart and bull.
And if that cart and bull turns over,
Papa's going to buy you a dog named Rover.

If that dog named Rover don't bark,
Papa's going to buy you a horse and cart.
And if that horse and cart falls down,
You'll still be the sweetest little baby in town.

Imitation

An Imitation rhyme introduces a moderate level of action, such as
pointing to oneself or other things around you or just clapping
hands. These rhymes are grouped into three loose categories. The
first six are good candidates for hello songs (first two) and good-bye
songs (next four). Following those are a group of rhymes which are all
"self-identification" rhymes, naming various parts of the body in the
verse. The last group are pretend rhymes, about animals, nature, or
doing things around the house. The last three of these are in foreign
languages and are challenging, but fun.

HELLO SONG (B) ♪
(Melody provided on page 111)

Hello everybody,	Wave hand.
And how are you,	Point to baby.
How are you,	Point to baby.
How are you?	Point to baby.
Hello everybody,	Wave hand.
And how are you,	Point to baby.
How are you today?	

HELLO SONG II (B) ♪
(Melody provided on page 111)

Hello, hello,	Wave hand and point to baby.
Hello and how are you?	
I'm fine, I'm fine,	Point to self.
And I hope that you are, too.	Point to baby.

THANK YOU RHYME (B)

Our hands say thank you	Hold hands up.
With a clap, clap, clap;	Clap hands.
Our feet say thank you	Point to feet.
With a tap, tap, tap.	Stamp or tap feet.
Clap, clap, clap;	Clap hands.
Tap, tap, tap.	Tap feet.
We roll our hands around,	Roll hands.
And say, "Good-bye."	Wave good-bye.

MY EYES CAN SEE (B)

My eyes can see.	Point to eyes.
My mouth can talk.	Point to mouth.
My ears can hear.	Point to ears.
My feet can walk.	Point to feet.
But when the clock	Point to clock or watch.
Its time does show,	
I'll take my rhymes	
And away I'll go.	Wave good-bye.

MYSELF (B)

On my face I have a nose,	Point to nose.
And way down here I have ten toes.	Point to toes.
I have two eyes that I can blink.	Point to eyes.
I have a head to help me think.	Point to head.
I have a chin and very near,	Point to chin.
I have two ears to help me hear.	Point to ears.
I have a mouth with which to speak,	Point to mouth.
And when I run I use my feet.	Point to feet.
Here are arms to hold up high,	Hold up arms.
And here's a hand to wave good-bye.	Wave hand.

TOUCH YOUR HEAD (B)

Touch your head,	Touch head.
Then your knee,	Touch knees.
Up to your shoulders,	Touch shoulders.
Like this you see.	
Reach for the ceiling,	Stretch arms up.
Touch the floor,	Crouch to floor.
That's all now,	Hold palms out.
There isn't any more.	Shake head.

WHERE IS THUMBKINS (W) ♪
(*Melody:* "Frère Jacques"—*traditional*)

Where is Thumbkins, Where is Thumbkins?	Hide hands behind back.
Here he comes,	Bring hands to front.
Here he comes.	Thumbs up.
Mighty glad to see you, Mighty glad to see you.	Wiggle thumbs at each other.
There he goes, There he goes.	Hands behind back again.

FE, FI, FO, FUM (W)

Fe, fi, fo, fum,	Clap to words.
See my fingers,	Wiggle fingers.
See my thumb.	Hold up thumb.
Fe, fi, fo, fum,	Clap to words.
Good-bye fingers,	One hand behind back.
Good-bye thumb.	Other hand behind back.

OPEN, SHUT THEM (B) ♪
(*Melody provided on page 119*)

Open, shut them, open, shut them,	Open and close fist and clap.
Give a little clap, clap, clap.	
Open, shut them, open, shut them,	
Put them in your lap, lap, lap.	
Creep them, creep them,	Walk hands up your or baby's
Creep them, creep them,	chest.
Right up to your chin.	
Open up your little mouth,	
But do not put them in.	Hide hands behind back.

The following two rhymes are fun for parent to use at home while dressing and bathing their babies.

PUT YOUR FINGER ON YOUR SHIRT (B) ♪
(*Melody:* "If You're Happy and You Know It"—*provided on page 114*)

Put your finger on your shirt,
On your shirt.
Put your finger on your shirt,
On your shirt.
Put your finger on your shirt,
Put your finger on your shirt,
Put your finger on your shirt,
Oh, on your shirt.

On your socks. . .

On your shoes. . .

On your pants. . .

Point to item of clothing as you sing about it, or encourage adults to point to clothing on baby.

PUT YOUR FINGER ON YOUR NOSE (B) ♪
(Melody: "If You're Happy and You Know It"—*provided on page 114)*

Put your finger on your nose,
On your nose.
Put your finger on your nose,
On your nose.
Put your finger on your nose,
Put your finger on your nose,
Put your finger on your nose,
Oh, your nose.

On your belly. . .

On your head. . .

Point to the part of the face
as you sing about it.

I WIGGLE MY FINGERS (B) ♪
(Melody: "Pop Goes the Weasel"—*traditional)*

I wiggle my fingers,
I wiggle my toes,
I wiggle my shoulders,
I wiggle my nose.

Wiggle fingers.
Point to toes.
Shrug shoulders.
Touch nose with finger.

Now no more wiggles
Are left in me,
So I will be still,
As still as can be.

Shake head "no."

Make "all gone" motion,
bring hands together, fold
in lap.

WIGGLE, WIGGLE FINGERS (B)

Wiggle, wiggle fingers,
Right up to the sky.
Wiggle, wiggle fingers,
Wave them all good-bye.

Wiggle fingers.
Raise hands.
Wiggle fingers.
Wave good-bye.

Wiggle, wiggle fingers,
Right into a ball.
Now throw them in your lap,
But do not let them fall.

Wiggle fingers.
Fold fingers into ball and
throw in lap, shake head
"no."

WITH OUR HANDS (W)

With our hands,	
We clap, clap, clap.	Clap hands.
With our feet,	
We stamp, stamp, stamp.	Stamp feet.
We hop three times,	
As high as can be,	Hop up and down.
And then we say,	
"Hey, look at me."	Point to self.

I HAVE TEN FINGERS (B)

I have ten fingers,	Hold up ten fingers.
And they all belong to me.	
I can make them do things,	
Would you like to see?	Point to baby.
I can put them up high,	Raise hands up.
I can put them down low,	Lower hands.
I can make them hide,	Put behind back.
And I can fold them so.	Fold them on lap.

THEY'RE A PART OF ME (W) ♪
(Melody: "The Wheels on the Bus"*—provided on page 121)*

Clap your hands, now,	Do appropriate actions as
Just like this,	indicated.
Just like this,	
Just like this.	
Clap your hands, now,	
Just like this,	
Clapping you and me.	
Stamp your feet. . .	
Jump on your legs. . .	
Shake your hands. . .	

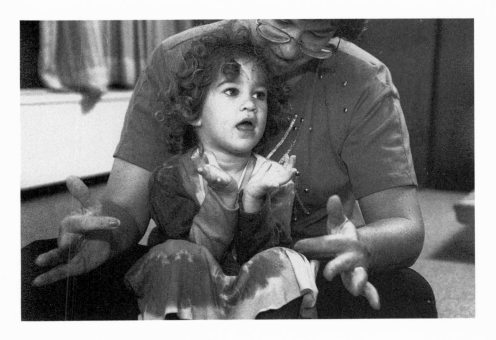

COME A LOOK A SEE (W) ♪
(Melody provided on page 109)

Come a look a see,	Wiggle thumb.
Here's my mom.	
Come a look a see,	Wiggle pointer.
Here's my pop.	
Come a look a see,	Wiggle middle finger.
Brother tall.	
Sister, baby,	Wiggle ring finger, pinkie.
I love them all.	Fold hand, kiss thumb.

I HEAR THUNDER (W) ♪
(Melody: "Frère Jacques"*—traditional)*

I hear thunder, I hear thunder,	Pretend to listen.
Hark, don't you? Hark, don't you?	Point to baby.
Pitter-patter raindrops,	Make rain with fingers.
Pitter-patter raindrops.	
I'm wet through,	Point to self.
So are you.	Point to baby.

WASH THE DISHES (W)

Wash the dishes,
Wipe the dishes,

Rub hands together in
circular motion.

Ring the bell for tea.

Shake fist back and forth.

Three good wishes,
Three good kisses,
I will give to thee.

Hold up three fingers.
Kiss baby or throw kisses to
baby.

PEASE PORRIDGE HOT (B)

Pease porridge hot,
Pease porridge cold.
Pease porridge in the pot,
Nine days old.
Some like it hot,
Some like it cold.
Some like it in the pot,
Nine days old.

Clap hands in rhythm to the
words.

PITTER PATTER (W)

Pitter patter falls the rain,
On the roof and window pane.
Softly, softly, it comes down,
Makes a stream that runs around.

Flutter fingers down for rain.

Place hands together and
move them like a moving
stream.

Flowers lift their heads and say,
"A nice cool drink for us today."

Cup hands together to form
flowers.

GRANDMA'S GLASSES (B)

These are Grandma's glasses.

Bring index finger and
thumb together to form
glasses on face.

This is Grandma's hat.

This is the way
She folds her hands,
And lays them on her lap.

Bring finger tips together in
a peak over head.
Fold hands and place on lap.

FIVE LITTLE PUMPKINS (W) ♪
(*Melody provided, on page 110*)

Five little pumpkins,
Sitting on a gate.
The first one said,
"Oh my, it's getting late."
The second one said,
"There are witches in the air."
The third one said,
"But I don't care."
The fourth one said,
"Let's run and run and run."
The fifth one said,
"I'm ready for some fun."

Hold up five fingers.

Hold up one finger.
Look at wrist.
Hold up two fingers.
"Ride a broom."
Hold up three fingers.
Shake head.
Hold up four fingers.
Arms in running motion.
Hold up five fingers.
Point to self.

Ooooh went the wind,
And out went the light.
And the five little pumpkins
Rolled out of sight.

Clap hands.
Hold up five fingers.
Roll hands.

THIS IS MY GARDEN (W)

This is my garden.
I'll rake it with care.
And then some flower seeds
I will plant there.
The sun will shine,
And the rain will fall.
And my garden will blossom,
Growing straight and tall.

Hold palm out.
Scratch fingers across palm.

Plant seeds on palm.
Hold arms above head.
Lower arms.
Unfold fingers slowly.

I SAW A LITTLE RABBIT (B)

I saw a little rabbit Go hop, hop, hop.	Make rabbit ears with two fingers; hop them on arm. Bend fingers on the word "flop".
I saw his long ears Go flop, flop, flop. I saw his little nose Go twink, twink, twink. I saw his little eyes Go wink, wink, wink. I said, "Little rabbit, Won't you stay?" But he looked at me, And hopped away.	Point to nose on "twink." Point to eyes on "wink." Have rabbit hop along arm again.

FIVE LITTLE MONKEYS (B) ♪
(*Melody provided on page 110*)

Five little monkeys, Jumping on the bed. One fell off, And bumped his head. Momma called the doctor, And the doctor said, "No more monkeys jumping on the bed!"	Hold up five fingers. Two fingers jump on palm of hand. Tap head lightly. Pretend to phone. Wag pointer finger.

Four little monkeys . . . etc.

HERE IS THE BEEHIVE (B)

Here is the beehive, Where are the bees? They're hiding inside, Where nobody sees. Watch them come out of the hive, One-two-three-four-five.	Hold up fist. Point to fist. Slowly unfold fingers.

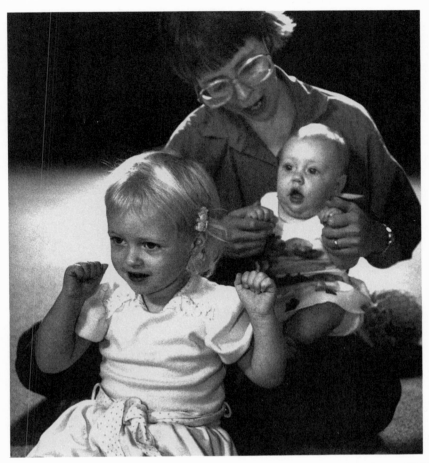

Although these next three rhymes would seem suited only to Walkers, they can be done for the Prewalkers' enjoyment without their needing to participate in the action.

TWO LITTLE BLACKBIRDS (B)

Two little blackbirds, Sitting on a hill. One named Jack, The other named Jill.	Hold up both fists with thumbs pointed up.
Fly away Jack, Fly away Jill. Come back Jack, Come back Jill.	Put one fist behind back; then the other fist. Then bring first back; then the other.

HERE'S A CUP (B)

Here's a cup,
And here's a cup,
And here's a pot of tea.

Pour one cup,
And pour the other cup,
And drink a cup with me.

Make circles with each hand
    for cups.
Bring hands together in big
    circle for pot.
Pour from one hand into the
    other, then pretend to
    drink.

FIVE PLUMP PEAS (B)

Five plump peas,
In a pea pod pressed.
One grew, two grew,
So did all the rest.
They grew, and they grew,
And they grew,
And never stopped.
They grew so fat,
The pea pod popped!

Put five fingers into a fist.

Reveal one finger at a time
    until all are straight up.
Then make a circle with both
    hands that gets bigger
    until the word "popped"—at
    which you clap hands.

WHEELS ON THE BUS (W) ♪
(*Melody provided on page 121*)

The wheels on the bus
Go round and round,
Round and round,
Round and round.
The wheels on the bus
Go round and round,
All over town.

Roll hands.

The wipers on the bus go
swish, swish. . .

Imitate wipers' swish, with
    forearms.

Change . . . clink, clink, clink.

Put money in other hand.

Driver . . . "Move on back."

Make pointing motion with
    thumb.

Babies . . . "Waa, waa, waa."	Pretend to rub eyes with fists.
Grown-ups . . . "Shh, shh, shh."	Put finger to lips.
Kids . . . yakkity, yak, yak.	Make talking motions with hand.
People . . . up and down.	Raise and lower self.
Wheels . . . round and round.	Roll hands.

ONCE I SAW A LITTLE BIRD (W)

Once I saw a little bird
Go hop, hop, hop.
And I cried, "Little bird,
Will you stop, stop, stop?"

Hold one palm out flat while
two fingers of other hand
hop across it.

I was going to the window
To say "How do you do?"
But he shook his little tail,
And far away he flew.

Pretend to shake hands.

Shake your tail.
Flap your wings.

PANCAKE (W)

Mix a pancake, stir a pancake,
Pop it in a pan.
Fry a pancake, toss a pancake,
Catch it if you can.

Pretend to stir.
Clap hands on "pop."
Pretend to fry, toss, and then
catch in hands.

GREEN LEAF (W)

Here's a green leaf,
And here's a green leaf,
And that you see makes two.
Here is a bud,
That makes a flower,
Watch it bloom for you.

Show palm.
Show other palm.

Close hands together.
Spread fingers, open hands,
keeping wrists joined.

HERE IS A BUNNY (W)

Here is a bunny
With ears so funny.
Here is his hole
In the ground.
When a noise he hears,
He pricks up his ears,
And jumps in his hole
In the ground.

Make fist with two fingers up
straight.
Make circle with fingers and
thumb of other hand.
Rotate rabbit as if hearing
noise.
Jump rabbit ears into hole.

FIVE KITTENS IN THE BED (W) ♪
(Melody provided on page 109)

Five kittens in the bed, And the little one said, "I'm crowded, roll over."	Hold up five fingers. Hunch shoulders together as if crowded.
So they all rolled over, And one fell out.	Roll hands. Hold up one finger.
Four kittens in the bed, And the little one said. . .	Hold up four fingers.
Three kittens in the bed, And the little one said. . .	Hold up three fingers.
Two kittens in the bed, And the little one said. . .	Hold up two fingers.
One kitten in the bed, And the little one said, "I'm lonely." So they all jumped in, And the little one said, "All right, good night!"	Hold up one finger.

EENSY, WEENSY SPIDER (W) ♪
(Melody traditional)

The eensy, weensy spider
Went up the water spout.
Down came the rain,
And washed the spider out.
Out came the sun,
And dried up all the rain.
And the eensy, weensy spider
Went up the spout again.
	Hands imitate spider while
	  rising in air.
	Lower hands, wiggle fingers.
	
	Arms in circle over head.
	
	Hands imitate spider while
	  rising up in air again.

The next four rhymes are foreign-language rhymes, which can be fun to include but should always be surrounded by very familiar rhymes. The first two are "self rhymes" while the others are pretend rhymes. We've included a phonetic spelling beneath each line. Check any standard English dictionary to help you follow the pronunciation guides.

JAPANESE GAME (W)

Hana, hana, hana, kuchi
(hänä, hänä, hänä, kōōchē)
Kuchi, kuchi, kuchi, mimi.
(kōōchē, kōōchē, kōōchē, mēmē)
Mimi, mimi, mimi, me.
(mēmē, mēmē, mēmē, mä)

Nose, nose, nose, mouth.
Mouth, mouth, mouth, ear.
Ear, ear, ear, eye.

Point to each feature as you say its name, first the Japanese version, then the English translation.

HEAD, SHOULDERS, KNEES AND TOES IN FRENCH (W) ♪
(Melody provided on page 111)

Tete, epaules, genoux et pieds,
(tĕt, āpōl, zhĕno͞o ā pyĕd)
Genoux et pieds.
(zhĕno͞o ā pyĕd)
Tete, epaules, genoux et pieds,
(tĕt, āpōl, zhĕno͞o ā pyĕd)
Genoux et pieds.
(zhĕno͞o ā pyĕd)

J'ai un nex, deux yeux,
(zhā œn nā, dœz yœ)
Deux oreilles et une bouche.
(dœz ərī ĕt ün bo͞och)
Tete, epaules, genoux et pieds,
(tĕt, āpōl, zhĕno͞o ā pyĕd)
Genoux et pieds.
(zhĕno͞o ā pyĕd)

Head, shoulders, knees and toes,
Knees and toes,
Head, shoulders, knees and toes,
Knees and toes.
I've a nose, two eyes,
Two ears and a mouth.
Head, shoulders, knees and toes,
Knees and toes.

Touch body parts in same
order as English
translation.

SPANISH CHOCOLATE RHYME (W)

Uno, dos, tres, cho-
(o͞onō, dōs, trās, chō-)
Uno, dos, tres, co-
(o͞onō, dōs, trās, kō-)
Uno, dos, tres, la-
(o͞onō, dōs, trās, lä-)
Uno, dos, tres, te-

Count out three fingers on
each line.

(o͞ono, dōs, trās, tā-)
Bate, Bate, chocolate.   Make stirring motion.
(bätä, bätä, chōkōlätä)

Since "bate" means to stir, you make stirring motions on the last line.

GERMAN GAME (W)

Eins, zwei, Polizei.   Touch thumbs.
(īnz, zvī, pō-letz-ī)
Drei, vier, offizier.   Touch pointers.
(dri, fēr, ôf-īts-zēr)
Funf, sechs, alter Hex.   Touch middle fingers.
(fo͞onf, zĕks, älter hĕx)
Sieben, acht, gute nacht.   Touch ring fingers.
(zēbĕn, äkht, gootä näkht)
Neun, zehn, auf wiedersehn.   Touch pinkies.
(noin, zān, ouf vēderzän)

One, two, policeman blue.
Three, four, captain of the corps.
Five, six, a witch on stick.
Seven, eight, the hour is late.
Nine, ten, till we meet again.

Activity

For the most active and physically independent babies, these rhymes usually involve the whole body, with actions like walking, jumping, or turning around. But as with any general statement, there are exceptions, as is apparent in the first three rhymes introduced here. The first two, "Up, Up, Up" and "The Noble Duke of York," are our "flying-baby songs" for the Prewalkers, as the adults help the Prewalkers up and down by lifting and lowering them on cue. The "Exercises" chant can be used with babies not ready to stretch their arms on their own, by having their adults gently help them to stretch. These are followed by three marching songs that can fit a variety of circumstances. Next are a group of "pretend" songs and rhymes, fun for use in the program and for baby to do at home and, lastly, a group of songs and rhymes dealing with "self."

UP, UP, UP (B) ♪
(Melody provided on page 121)

Here we go up, up, up,
Here we go down, down, down.
Here we go up, up, up,
Here we go down, down, down.

Raise and lower arms or baby as indicated.

NOBLE DUKE OF YORK (B) ♪
(Melody provided on page 117)

Oh, the noble Duke of York,
He had ten thousand men.
He marched them up
to the top of the hill,
And marched them down again.

And when they're up, they're up,
And when they're down, they're down.
And when they're only half way up,
They're neither up nor down.

March in place or gently bounce baby.
Raise and lower arms or baby throughout the song as the words indicate.

EXERCISES (B)

Exercise, exercises,
Let's all do our exercises.
Exercises, exercises,
Let's all do our exercises.

Stretch your arms or baby's
arms out to side or above
head as you say the words.

These next three songs can be done as marching-into-the-program songs or as general marching songs with pretended motions as the words indicate.

DOWN BY THE STATION (W) ♪
(*Melody provided on page 109*)

Down by the station,
Early in the morning.
See the little puffer-bellies,
All in a row.

See the station master,
Pull the little handle.
Chug, chug, toot, toot,
Off we go.

TWO BY TWO (W) ♪
(Melody provided on page 120)

Walking along two by two,
Walking along two by two.
Walking along two by two,
Skip to my Lou, my darling.

Everyone's welcome, you come too,
Everyone's welcome, you come too.
Everyone's welcome, you come too,
Skip to my Lou, my darling.

Walk around in a circle or in place with adults holding their children's hands.

MARCHING SONG (W) ♪
(Melody: "If You're Happy and You Know It"*—provided on page 114)*

Let's march together,
You and me.
Let's march together,
You and me.
I'll march with you
And you'll march with me.
Let's march together,
You and me.

March in place or in a circle.

MULBERRY BUSH (W) ♪
(Melody traditional)

Here we go round the mulberry
    bush,
The mulberry bush, the mulberry
    bush.

Walk in circle.

Here we go round the mulberry
   bush,
So early in the morning.
This is the way we wash our   Stand in place and pretend
   hands,   to wash hands.
Wash our hands, wash our hands.
This is the way we wash our
   hands,
So early in the morning.

Wash our clothes. . .   Pretend to wash clothes.

Hang them up. . .   Pretend to hang clothes.

TEDDY BEAR, TEDDY BEAR (W)

Teddy bear, Teddy bear,   Do actions as indicated.
Turn around.
Teddy bear, Teddy bear,
Touch the ground.
Teddy bear, Teddy bear,
Show your shoe.
Teddy bear, Teddy bear,
That will do.
Teddy bear, Teddy bear,
Go to bed.
Teddy bear, Teddy bear,
Rest your head.
Teddy bear, Teddy bear,
Turn out the light.
Teddy bear, Teddy bear,
Say goodnight.

The following can be used as circle games or as simple songs with no
motions, changing the color of the bird that you see, or pretend to
see, with baby.

HERE STANDS A REDBIRD (W) ♪
(Melody provided on page 112)

Here stands a redbird,
Tra-la-la-la-la.
Here stands a redbird,
Tra-la-la-la-la.
Let's see what he does.

Stand up for the first verse.

Here hops a redbird. . .

Hop up and down.

Here flaps a redbird. . .

Flap arms.

BLUE BIRD, BLUE BIRD (W) ♪
(Melody provided on page 108)

Blue bird, blue bird,
Through my window.
Blue bird, blue bird,
Through my window.
Blue bird, blue bird,
Through my window.
Oh, Mommy, I am happy.

MISTER SUN (W) ♪
(Melody provided on page 117)

Oh, Mister Sun, Sun,
Mister Golden Sun,
Please shine down on me.
Oh, Mister Sun, Sun,
Mister Golden Sun,
Hiding behind a tree.
These little children
Are asking you
To please come out
So we can play with you.
Oh Mister Sun, Sun,
Mister Golden Sun,
Please shine down on me.

Hold arms above head in a
circle, then lower arms;
point to self.
Hold arms above head in a
circle.
Put hands in front of face.
Point to others in group;
beckon with arm

Hold arms above head in
circle.
Lower arms and point to self.

LITTLE LEAVES (W) ♪
(Melody: "London Bridge"—*traditional)*

Little leaves fall	Flutter hands down.
Gently down.	
Red and yellow	
Orange and brown.	
Whirling, whirling,	Turn self around.
Round and round,	
Down, down, down.	Sit, crouch, or flutter hands down.

SNOWMAN (W) ♪
(Melody: "Mulberry Bush"—*traditional)*

Roll him and roll him,	Roll hands.
Until he is big.	
Roll him until he is	
Fat as a pig.	
He has two eyes,	Point to eyes.
And a hat on his head.	Place hand on head.
He'll stand there all night,	Stand at attention.
While we go to bed.	Rest head on folded hands.

LITTLE BROWN SEED (W)

I'm a little brown seed,	Crouch down.
Rolled up in a tiny ball.	
The rain and the sunshine	Rise up.
Will make me big and tall.	Reach arms over head.

RING AROUND THE ROSIE (W) ♪
(Melody traditional)

Ring around the rosie,	Hold baby's hands and walk in circle.
A pocket full of posies.	
Hush-a, hush-a,	
We all fall down.	Crouch down.

Pulling up the daisies,	Pretend to pick flowers.
Pulling up the daisies.	
Hush-a, hush-a,	
We all stand up.	Stand up.

LITTLE TEAPOT (W) ♪
(*Melody traditional*)

I'm a little teapot,	Stand still.
Short and stout.	
Here is my handle,	Put hand on hip.
Here is my spout.	Extend other arm.
When I get all steamed up,	
Hear me shout,	
"Just tip me over,	Bend to side of extended
And pour me out."	arm.

COLORS GAME (W) ♪
(*Melody:* "Did You Ever See a Lassie"—*traditional*)

If you have a (color) shirt on,
Please stand up, please stand up.
If you have a (color) shirt on,
Stand up right now.

Insert any color as needed.

IF YOU'RE HAPPY AND YOU KNOW IT (W) ♪
(*Melody provided on page 114*)

If you're happy and you know it,	
Clap your hands.	Clap, clap.
If you're happy and you know it,	
Clap your hands.	Clap, clap.
If you're happy and you know it,	
And you really want to show it,	
If you're happy and you know it,	
Clap your hands.	Clap, clap.

Other verses can be added, such as "Blow me a kiss" or "Give yourself a hug."

HEAD, SHOULDERS, KNEES AND TOES (W) ♪
(Melody provided on page 111)

Head, shoulders, knees and toes,	Touch parts of body as
Knees and toes.	indicated.
Head, shoulders, knees and toes,	
Knees and toes.	
I've a nose, two eyes,	
Two ears and a mouth.	
Head, shoulders, knees and toes,	
Knees and toes.	

SING WITH ME (W) ♪
(Melody: "Mulberry Bush"—*traditional)*

Come along and sing with me,
Sing with me, sing with me.
Come along and sing with me,
So early in the morning.

Come along and clap with me. . .   Clap hands.

Come along and stretch with   Raise arms.
   me. . .

Come along and march with   March in place.
   me. . .

I HAVE A LITTLE HEART (W)

I have a little heart,   Put hand over heart.
And it goes thump, thump,   Pat three times.
   thump.
It keeps right on beating,
When I jump, jump, jump.   Jump three times.

I get a special feeling,
When I look at you.   Point to baby.
It makes me want to give you
A kiss or two.   Blow kisses.

QUIET-TIME RHYME (W)

I'll touch my hair,   Touch hair.
My lips, my eyes.   Touch lips, eyes.
I'll sit up straight,   Sit up.
And then I'll rise.   Stand up.
I'll touch my ears,   Touch ears.
My nose, my chin.   Touch nose, chin.
Then, quietly,
Sit down again.   Sit down again.

SOMETIMES I AM TALL (W)

Sometimes I am tall,	Stand up straight.
Sometimes I am small.	Crouch down.
Sometimes I am very, very tall,	Stretch on tip toes.
Sometimes I am very, very small.	Crouch down.
Sometimes tall,	Stand up.
Sometimes small.	Crouch down.
See how I am now.	Stand normally.

ROLL YOUR HANDS (W) ♪
(*Melody:* "Row, Row, Your Boat"—*traditional*)

Roll, roll, roll your hands,	Roll hands as song indicates.
As fast as fast can be.	
Do it now, let me see,	
Do it now with me.	
Clap, clap, clap your hands,	Clap hands as song
As loud as loud can be.	indicates.
Do it now, let me see,	
Do it now with me.	
Tap, tap, tap your feet,	Tap feet as song indicates.
As softly as can be.	
Do it now, let me see,	
Do it now with me.	
Shake, shake, shake your feet,	Shake feet as song indicates.
As quickly as can be.	
Do it now, let me see,	
Do it now with me.	
Roll, roll, roll your hands,	Roll hands as song indicates.
As fast, as fast can be.	
Do it now, let me see,	
Do it now with me.	

CLAP, CLAP, CLAP YOUR HANDS (W) ♪
(*Melody provided on page 108*)

Clap, clap, clap your hands, Clap them just like me. Clap, clap, clap your hands, Clap them just like me.	Clap hands in rhythm to the song.
Touch, touch, touch your shoulders, Touch them just like me. Touch, touch, touch your shoulders, Touch them just like me.	Touch shoulders in rhythm to song.
Tap, tap, tap your knees, Tap them just like me. Tap, tap, tap your knees, Tap them just like me.	Tap knees in rhythm to the song.
Shake, shake, shake your head, Shake it just like me. Shake, shake, shake your head, Shake it just like me.	Shake head in rhythm to the song.

TWO LITTLE FEET (W) ♪
(*Melody:* "Baa, Baa Black Sheep"—*traditional*)

Two little feet go tap, tap, tap, Two little hands go clap, clap, clap. A quiet little leap up from my chair, Two little arms reach high in the air. Two little feet go tap, tap, tap, Two little hands go clap, clap, clap.	Do appropriate actions as indicated.

BEND AND STRETCH (W) ♪
(Melody provided on page 108)

Bend and stretch so way up high,
Stand on tiptoe, touch the sky.

Bend and stretch and see me
   grow,
I'm so tall from head to toe.

Stand up and reach arms as
   high as you can.

Stand and touch head and
   then feet.

I'M GROWING (W) ♪
(Melody provided on page 114)

I'm growing, I'm growing,
I'm growing up all over.
I'm growing here, I'm growing
   there,
I'm just growing everywhere.

As you sing, point to arms,
   legs, or whatever seems
   appropriate.

LITTLE BABY DEAR (W) ♪
(Melody provided on page 115)

Clap your hands, little Baby,
Clap your hands, little Baby Dear.
Clap your hands, little Baby,
Clap 'em, Baby Dear.

This is a good song in which to substitute individual children's
names for "Baby". Change the action to whatever suits the occasion,
such as, "Jump around, little Matthew" or "Stamp your feet, little
Sally."

I PUT MY ARMS UP HIGH (W)

I put my arms up high,
I put my arms down low.
I put my arms real stiff,
Then I let them go.

Arms over head.
Arms at side.
Arms straight out.
Drop arms down.

First I swing like this,   Swing to one side.
Then I swing like that.   Swing to other side.
Then make my arms real round,   Make circle with arms.
And then I make them flat.   Drop arms to side.

PART III
RESOURCES

Evaluation Form For Mother Goose Time

1. How did you hear about Mother Goose Time?
2. Is this the first Mother Goose Time you have attended?
3. How many sessions have you previously attended?
4. Did you repeat some of the songs or finger plays at home?
5. If your child is able to speak, did he or she talk about the program while at home?
6. If the child has older siblings, did they attend Mother Goose Time? Why/Why not?
7. What did your child enjoy most about the program?
8. What did you enjoy most about the program?
9. What do you think should be eliminated from the program?
10. What do you think should be included that was not?
11. Has your child shown increased interest in books since attending Mother Goose Time?
12. How many books do you and your child share each week?

13. Has that number increased since attending Mother Goose Time?
14. How often do you visit the library other than for Mother Goose Time sessions?
15. Is another time or day more convenient for you to attend Mother Goose Time?

Music Appendix

All the Pretty Little Horses

Hush - a - bye, don't you cry, Go to sleep - y, lit - tle ba - by.

When you wake, you shall have All the pret - ty lit - tle hors - es.

Blacks and bays, dap - ples and grays All the pret - ty lit - tle hors - es.

Hush - a - bye, don't you cry, Go to sleep - y, lit - tle ba - by.

Baby A-Go Go

Ba - by a - go - go, Hey - ah! Ba - by a -

go - go, Hey - ah! Ba - by a - go - Oh! Ba - by a - go - go - go!

Bend and Stretch

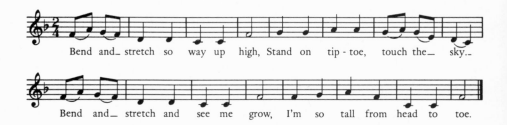

Bend and_ stretch so way up high, Stand on tip-toe, touch the_ sky._

Bend and_ stretch and see me grow, I'm so tall from head to toe.

Blue Bird, Blue Bird

Blue bird, blue bird, Through my win-dow. Blue bird, blue bird, Through my win-dow.

Blue bird, blue bird, Through my win-dow. Oh, Mom-my, I am hap-py.

Clap Hands

Clap hands, clap hands, Till Dad-dy comes home.

Clap hands, clap hands, Till Mom-my comes home.

Clap, Clap, Clap Your Hands

Clap, clap, clap your hands, Clap them just like me.

Clap, clap, clap your hands, Clap them just like me.

Come a Look a See

Come- a - look - a - see, Here's my mom. Come- a - look- a - see, Here's my pop.

Come- a - look - a - see, Broth - er tall. Sis - ter, ba - by, I love them all.

Down by the Station

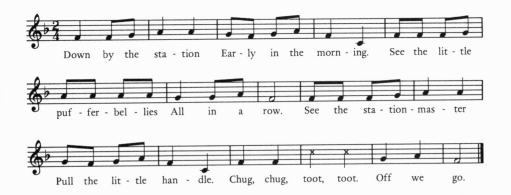

Down by the sta - tion Ear - ly in the morn - ing. See the lit - tle

puf - fer - bel - lies All in a row. See the sta - tion - mas - ter

Pull the lit - tle han - dle. Chug, chug, toot, toot. Off we go.

Five Kittens in the Bed

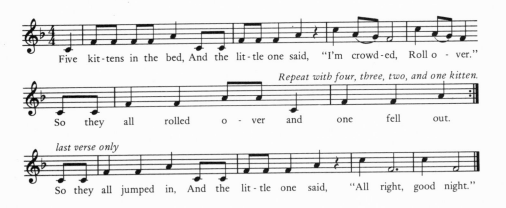

Five kit - tens in the bed, And the lit - tle one said, "I'm crowd - ed, Roll o - ver."

Repeat with four, three, two, and one kitten.

So they all rolled o - ver and one fell out.

last verse only

So they all jumped in, And the lit - tle one said, "All right, good night."

Five Little Monkeys

Five lit - tle mon - keys Jump - ing on the bed. One fell off and

Bumped his head. Mom - ma called the doc - tor And the doc - tor said,

Spoken: "No more monkeys
Jumping on the bed!"

Five Little Pumpkins

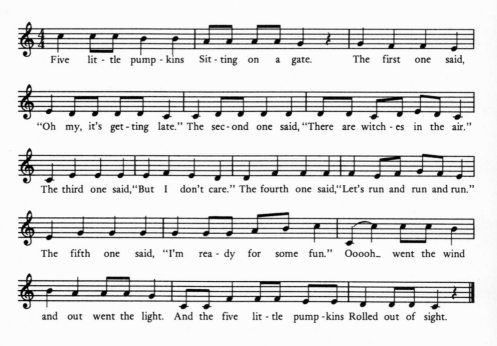

Five lit - tle pump - kins Sit - ting on a gate. The first one said,

"Oh my, it's get - ting late." The sec - ond one said, "There are witch - es in the air."

The third one said, "But I don't care." The fourth one said, "Let's run and run and run."

The fifth one said, "I'm rea - dy for some fun." Ooooh_ went the wind

and out went the light. And the five lit - tle pump - kins Rolled out of sight.

Head, Shoulders, Knees and Toes

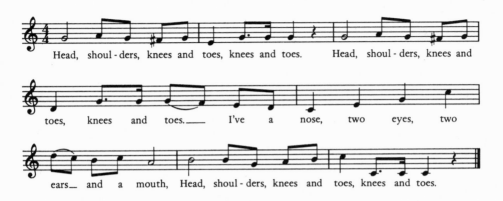

Hello Song

Hello Song II

Here Stands a Redbird

Here stands a red-bird, Tra-la-la-la-la-la. Here stands a red-bird,

Tra-la-la-la-la. Let's see what he does.

Hey Diddle Diddle

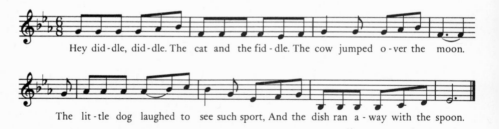

Hey did-dle, did-dle. The cat and the fid-dle. The cow jumped o-ver the moon.

The lit-tle dog laughed to see such sport, And the dish ran a-way with the spoon.

Hickory Dickory Dock

Hick-o-ry, dick-o-ry, dock.__ The mouse ran up the clock.__

The clock struck one, And down he run. Hick-o-ry, dick-o-ry, dock.

Hot Cross Buns

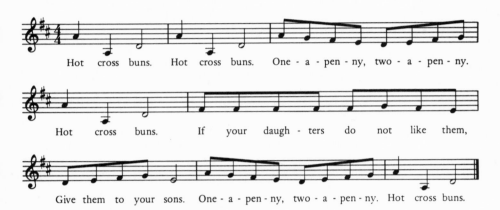

Hot cross buns. Hot cross buns. One - a - pen - ny, two - a - pen - ny.

Hot cross buns. If your daugh - ters do not like them,

Give them to your sons. One - a - pen - ny, two - a - pen - ny. Hot cross buns.

Humpty Dumpty

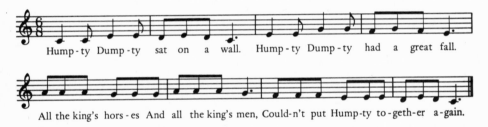

Hump - ty Dump - ty sat on a wall. Hump - ty Dump - ty had a great fall.

All the king's hors - es And all the king's men, Could - n't put Hump - ty to - geth - er a - gain.

If You're Happy and You Know It

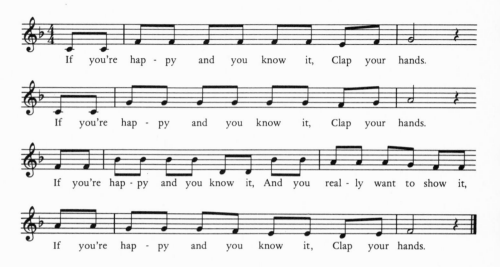

If you're hap - py and you know it, Clap your hands.

If you're hap - py and you know it, Clap your hands.

If you're hap - py and you know it, And you real - ly want to show it,

If you're hap - py and you know it, Clap your hands.

I'm Growing

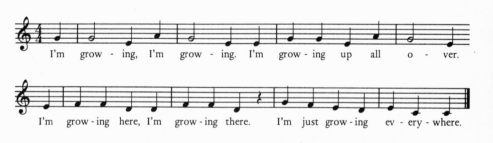

I'm grow - ing, I'm grow - ing. I'm grow - ing up all o - ver.

I'm grow - ing here, I'm grow - ing there. I'm just grow - ing ev - ery - where.

Lavender's Blue

Lav - en - der's blue, dil - ly dil - ly, Lav - en - der's green.

When I am king, dil - ly dil - ly, You shall be queen.

Who told you so, dil - ly dil - ly, Who told you so?

'Twas my own heart, dil - ly dil - ly, That told me so.

Little Baby Dear

Clap your hands, lit - tle Ba - by. Clap your hands, lit - tle Ba - by Dear.

Clap your hands, lit - tle Ba - by. Clap 'em, Ba - by Dear.

Little Boy Blue

Lit - tle boy blue, Come blow__ your horn. The sheep's in the mead - ow, The cow's in the corn. But where's the boy Who looks af - ter the sheep? He's un - der the hay - stack, Fast__ a - sleep. Will__ you wake him? No,__ not I, For if I do, He's sure__ to cry.

Little Jack Horner

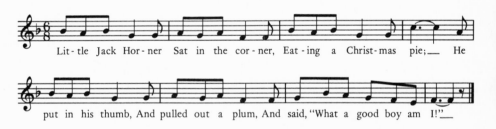

Lit - tle Jack Hor - ner Sat in the cor - ner, Eat - ing a Christ - mas pie;__ He put in his thumb, And pulled out a plum, And said, "What a good boy am I!"__

Mister Sun

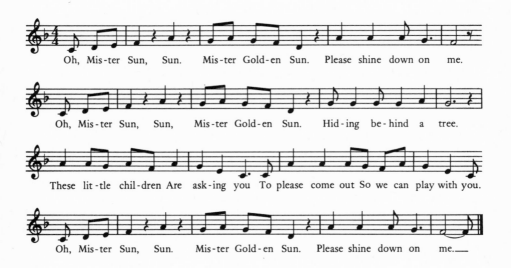

Oh, Mis-ter Sun, Sun. Mis-ter Gold-en Sun. Please shine down on me.

Oh, Mis-ter Sun, Sun, Mis-ter Gold-en Sun. Hid-ing be-hind a tree.

These lit-tle chil-dren Are ask-ing you To please come out So we can play with you.

Oh, Mis-ter Sun, Sun. Mis-ter Gold-en Sun. Please shine down on me.___

Noble Duke of York

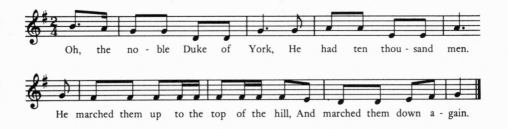

Oh, the no - ble Duke of York, He had ten thou - sand men.

He marched them up to the top of the hill, And marched them down a - gain.

Oh, Baby

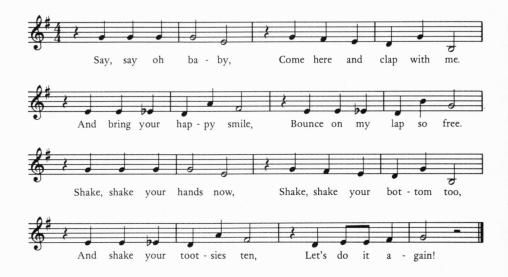

Say, say oh ba - by, Come here and clap with me.

And bring your hap - py smile, Bounce on my lap so free.

Shake, shake your hands now, Shake, shake your bot - tom too,

And shake your toot - sies ten, Let's do it a - gain!

Old Mother Goose

Old Moth - er Goose, when she want - ed to wan - der, would

ride through the air on a ver - y fine___ gan - der;

Old Fa - ther Gan - der, when the wind was fast and loose, would

ride through the air on a ver - y fine goose.

Open, Shut Them

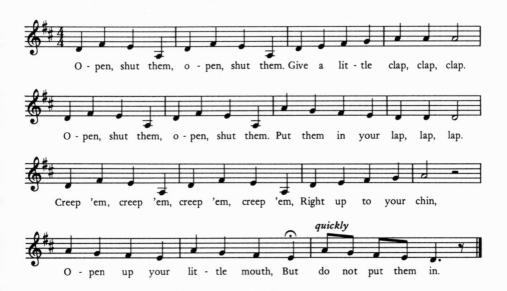

O - pen, shut them, o - pen, shut them. Give a lit - tle clap, clap, clap.

O - pen, shut them, o - pen, shut them. Put them in your lap, lap, lap.

Creep 'em, creep 'em, creep 'em, creep 'em, Right up to your chin,

quickly

O - pen up your lit - tle mouth, But do not put them in.

Polly Put the Kettle On

Pol - ly put the ket - tle on. Pol - ly put the ket - tle on.

Pol - ly put the ket - tle on. We'll all have tea.

Su - key take it off a - gain. Su - key take it off a - gain.

Su - key take it off a - gain. They've all gone a - way.

Rain, Rain, Go Away

Rain, rain go a-way, Come a-gain some oth-er day. All these chil-dren want to play.

Ride a Cock Horse

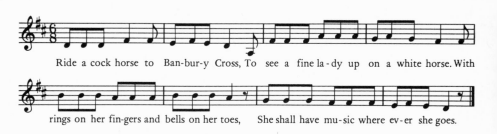

Ride a cock horse to Ban-bur-y Cross, To see a fine la-dy up on a white horse. With

rings on her fin-gers and bells on her toes, She shall have mu-sic where ev-er she goes.

To Market, To Market

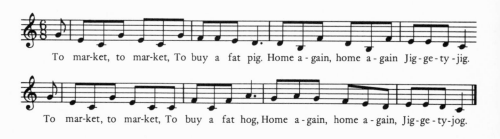

To mar-ket, to mar-ket, To buy a fat pig. Home a-gain, home a-gain Jig-ge-ty-jig.

To mar-ket, to mar-ket, To buy a fat hog, Home a-gain, home a-gain, Jig-ge-ty-jog.

Two by Two

Walk-ing a-long, two by two. Walk-ing a-long, two by two.

Walk-ing a-long, two by two. Skip to my Lou, my dar-ling.

Up, Up, Up

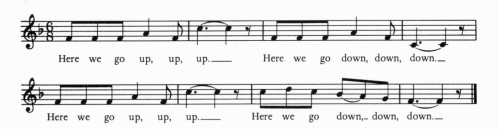

Here we go up, up, up.___ Here we go down, down, down.___

Here we go up, up, up.___ Here we go down,_ down, down.___

Wheels on the Bus

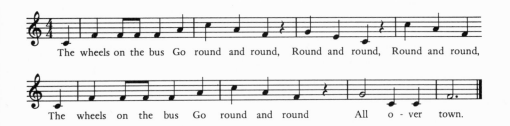

The wheels on the bus Go round and round, Round and round, Round and round,

The wheels on the bus Go round and round All o-ver town.

Display Books

There are many books in addition to the seventeen listed here that would contribute to a great display. These titles all share several essential elements: celebrating books and nursery rhymes and the importance of bringing them together for babies and their caregivers to enjoy.

Beatrix Potter's Nursery Rhyme Book. Illus. by Beatrix Potter. London: Frederick Warne, 1984.

A charming collection of traditional nursery rhymes decorated with figures, scenes, and sketches from various Potter works.

Brown, Marc. *Finger Rhymes.* Illus. by author. New York: Dutton, 1980.

Line drawings and simple, boxed diagrams make this collection of fourteen finger plays a delight for both baby and adult.

_____. *Hand Rhymes.* Illus. by author. New York: Dutton, 1985.

A sequel to *Finger Rhymes,* this book has fourteen more finger plays, some seasonal, some recognizable, all accompanied by watercolor illustrations.

Cousins, Lucy, ed. *The Little Dog Laughed and Other Nursery Rhymes.* illus. by editor. New York: Dutton, 1989.

More than fifty rhymes, some short, some long, all familiar and all fun; decorated with the childlike paintings of Lucy Cousins.

De Angeli, Marguerite, ed. *Marguerite de Angeli's Book of Nursery and Mother Goose Rhymes.* Illus. by editor. New York: Doubleday, 1953.

Still a classic with over 300 rhymes and 200 illustrations; a Caldecott Honor Book.

Knight, Joan. *Tickle-Toe Rhymes.* Illus. by John Wallner. New York: Orchard Books, 1988.

Thirteen different ways to do "This Little Pig" with matching illustrations.

Little Songs of Long Ago: A Collection of Favorite Poems and Rhymes. Illus. by Henriette Willebeek Le Mair. New York: Philomel, 1988.

A lovely new edition of a book first published in 1912, this is a companion volume to *Our Old Nursery Rhymes* and is a collection of classic and familiar nursery rhymes and songs, beautifully decorated with Le Mair's delicate illustrations.

Marcus, Leonard S., and Amy Schwartz. *Mother Goose's Little Misfortunes.* Illus. by Amy Schwartz. New York: Bradbury Press, 1990.

A celebration of all that is off-beat about Mother Goose, it highlights the rhymes that are comical, tragical but magical—all paired with wild and wacky watercolor illustrations.

Michael Foreman's Mother Goose. Illus. by Michael Foreman with foreword by Iona Opie. San Diego: Harcourt Brace Jovanovich, 1991.

More than a collection of classic rhymes, these witty watercolors contain intriguing visual hints for the watchful reader.

Our Old Nursery Rhymes: A Collection of Favorite Nursery Rhymes. Illus. by Henriette Willebeek Le Mair. New York: Philomel Books, 1989.

A new edition of a collection first published in 1911, it contains thirty traditional nursery rhymes decorated with soft, old-fashioned illustrations.

Opie, Iona, and Peter Opie. *Tail Feathers from Mother Goose: The Opie Rhyme Book.* Boston: Little Brown & Co., 1988.

Wonderful rhymes and lighthearted illustrations by various artists are sure to soothe the hearts and souls of readers everywhere.

Plotz, Helen, ed. *A Week of Lullabies.* Illus. Marisabina Russo. New York: Greenwillow, 1988.

A week's worth of rhymes, a week's worth of hugs, a week's worth of love. Share them with the nearest baby.

Polly Put the Kettle On and Other Rhymes. Photographs by Anthea Sieveking. London: Barrons Educational Series, 1991.

One of a series of four board books with Mother Goose rhymes and stunning photography to match, showing kids doing what they do best—playing! The other three books have animal rhymes, bedtime rhymes, and "splashy rhymes." A pure delight.

Prelutsky, Jack, comp. *Read-Aloud Rhymes for the Very Young.* Illus. by Marc Brown. New York: Alfred A. Knopf, 1986.

A collection of over 200 rhymes about all manner of things important to a child—from kittens to wishes to sweet dreams.

Rain, Rain, Go Away! A Book of Nursery Rhymes. Illus. by Jonathan Langley. New York: Dial Books for Young Readers, 1991.

Humorous and charming visual interpretations of many familiar and some not-so-familiar nursery rhymes.

Shott, Stephen. *Baby's World.* Photographs by Stephen Shott. New York: Dutton, 1980.

Sturdy pages present photographs of objects, all of them familiar and important to a baby's world. A must for any display meant to snare a tot's undivided attention.

Sieveking, Anthea. *What's Inside?* Photographs by author. New York: Dial Books for Young Readers, 1990.

It asks the question, "What's inside?" and provides clear photos on durable pages that help you answer. Each familiar object contains many brightly colored objects familiar to every baby. A sure winner.

Watson, Clyde. *Catch Me and Kiss Me and Say It Again.* Illus. by Wendy Watson. New York: Philomel, 1978.

Thirty-two original rhymes in the tradition of Mother Goose decorated with lighthearted, full-page illustrations.

Watson, Wendy. *Wendy Watson's Mother Goose.* Illus. by author. New York: Lothrop, Lee and Shepard, 1989.

A wonderful book for gift or display, this has a large gathering of short, classic verse illustrated in the delicate Watson style with a first-line index, subject index, and bibliography.

Suggested Picture-Book Titles for Mother Goose Time

This list represents a sampling of suitable picture books for use during a Mother Goose Time program. To a title, they all demonstrate the components of a good picture book for the very young: bold graphics, bright and pleasing colors, repetitive or rhyming words, simple plot or brief text, and a relatively large page size.

Brown, Margaret Wise. *Goodnight Moon.* Illus. by Clement Hurd. New York: Harper & Row, 1947.

> The standard by which all books for the very young can be judged, this has it all—color, cadence, and delicious sounds.

Cazet, Denys. *Mother Night.* Illus. by author. New York: Orchard Books, 1989.

> As Mother Night draws evening over the earth, animal parents bid their babies good night until it's time to wake them with morning kisses and stories.

Deming, Alhambra G. *Who Is Tapping at My Window?* Illus. by Monica Wellington. New York: Dutton, 1988.

> "Not I," says each animal until the rain finally admits to tapping on the child's windowpane.

Galdone, Paul. *Three Little Kittens.* Illus. by author. New York: Clarion, 1986.

> The traditional tale of the lost and found mittens accompanied by cozily cluttered illustrations of a charming cat family.

Hale, Sarah Josepha Buell. *Mary Had a Little Lamb.* Photographs and afterword by Bruce McMillan. New York: Scholastic, 1990.

> A bespectacled Mary in bright yellow overalls is followed by her doting lamb in this contemporary interpretation of the traditional rhyme.

Henderson, Kathy. *The Baby's Book of Babies.* Photographs by Anthea Sieveking. New York: Dial Books for Young Readers, 1989.

Real babies doing just what babies do—looking, strolling, splashing, laughing—babies, babies, everywhere!

Kamen, Gloria. *Paddle, Said the Swan.* Illus. by author. New York: Atheneum, 1989.

Rhythmic, rhyming verse describes the day's events through the sounds of animals and a cuddly baby boy.

Kightly, Rosalinda. *The Postman.* Illus. by author. New York: Macmillan, 1988.

Simple rhyming story of a postman's daily rounds to familiar neighborhood places.

Maris, Ron. *In My Garden.* Illus. by author. New York: Greenwillow, 1987.

Brief text and bright realistic drawings reveal the secrets of a young girl's garden.

Martin, Bill, Jr. *Brown Bear, Brown Bear, What Do You See?* Illus. by Eric Carle. New York: Holt, Rinehart and Winston, Inc., 1967, 1983.

Brightly colored collages of familiar animals accompany the mesmerizing sing-song text of this classic concept book.

———, and John Archambault. *Here Are My Hands.* Illus. by Ted Rand. New York: Holt, 1987.

Crayon-like drawings of multiracial children inventory various parts of the body and their possible uses—"my cheeks for kissing and blushing."

Ormerod, Jan. *The Saucepan Game.* Illus. by author. New York: Lothrop, Lee & Shepard, 1989.

Chubby-cheeked baby in a bright yellow sleeper plays with a shiny saucepan while a curious black-and-white cat watches.

Oxenbury, Helen. *All Fall Down.* Illus. by author. New York: Aladdin, 1987.

Round-faced, raisin-eyed toddlers rush across the pages of this oversized board book. This is one of four titles in a series noted for its multiracial representation and engaging text.

Shapiro, Arnold L. *Who Says That?* Illus. by Monica Wellington. New York: Dutton, 1991.

Brightly-colored animals make a variety of sounds in this simple poem.

Weiss, Nicki. *Where Does the Brown Bear Go?* Illus. by author. New York: Greenwillow, 1989.

Recognizable animals leap, fly, and walk across each page, leading a listening child along through this soothing, rhythmic verse.

Williams, Sue. *I Went Walking.* Illus. by Julie Vivas. San Diego: Gulliver Books, 1990.

Simple question-and-answer format follows a child on an animal-filled walk.

Wood, Don, and Audrey Wood. *Piggies*. San Diego: Harcourt Brace Jovanovich, 1991.

A lighthearted, winsome interpretation of the traditional finger play.

Resource Books

The following bibliography represents only a portion of the available collection from which to cull rhymes and songs. All the titles included have an extensive selection. Some have musical annotations and directions for parents and programmers, and many have wonderful illustrations. The tapes included are just a taste of what is available. They can be valuable resources whether you need to locate one or one hundred rhymes.

Baring-Gould, William and Cecil Baring-Gould, ed. *The Annotated Mother Goose.* Illus. by Caldecott, Crane, et al. New York: Clarkson-Potter, Inc., 1982.
> The ultimate collection for the Mother-Goose scholar; this has notes, histories, and rhymes aplenty.

Fowke, Edith. *Sally Go Round the Sun.* Illus. by Carlos Marchiori. Garden City: Doubleday, 1969.
> One of the classics, with three hundred children's songs, rhymes, and games, this is still a great source.

Fox, Dan, ed. *Go In and Out the Window: An Illustrated Songbook for Young People.* Illus. with art from Metropolitan Museum of Art. New York: Henry Hòlt & Co., 1987.
> A songbook not to be missed, filled with children's standards old and new, and decorated with beautiful art.

Glazer, Tom. *The Mother Goose Songbook.* Illus. by David McPhail. New York: Doubleday, 1990.
> Forty-four favorite Mother Goose rhymes with music for piano arranged with Glazer's style and illustrated with McPhail's bright, bold art.

Griego, Margo C., Betsy L. Bucks, Sharon Gilbert, and Laurel H. Kimball. *Tortillitas Para Mama and Other Nursery Rhymes/Spanish and English.* Illus. by Barbara Cooney. New York: Holt, Rinehart & Winston, 1981.
> Thirteen short, lovely finger play rhymes illustrated by the vibrant, colorful paintings of Barbara Cooney.

Hammett, Carol, and Elaine Beuffel. *Toddlers on Parade.* Audio cassette. Long Branch, N.J.: Kimbo Productions, 1985.

A fun and music-filled tape of songs and games for baby and toddler, perfect for adults and infants to share.

Hart, Jane, comp. *Singing Bee*. Illus. Anita Lobel. New York: Lothrop, Lee & Shepard Books, 1982.

A collection of favorite children's songs, charmingly illustrated, versatile enough for a variety of uses.

Hegner, Priscilla. *Baby Games: 6 Weeks to 1 Year*. Audio cassette. Long Branch, N.J.: Kimbo Productions, 1987.

Cuddly and quiet or bouncing and active, the songs and games on this tape are just right for listening and learning.

Jenkins, Ella. *The Ella Jenkins Songbook*. Illus. by Peggy Lipschutz. New York: Oak Publications, 1966.

A collection of twenty-six songs and chants with notes on their use, this book is by one of the foremost authorities on children's programming.

Larrick, Nancy, comp. *Songs from Mother Goose: with the Traditional Melody for Each*. Illus. by Nancy Larrick. New York: Harper & Row, 1989.

Simple musical arrangements and light, fanciful drawings decorate this collection of both favorite and little-known Mother Goose rhymes.

McGrath, Bob, and Kathryn Smithrim. *The Baby Record*. Audio Cassette. Toronto, Ontario: Kids' Records, 1983.

Bouncing rhymes, finger plays, instrument play, and lullabies, this is sure to soothe many a baby and parent.

Nichols, Judy. *Storytimes for Two-Year-Olds*. Illus. by Lora Sears. Chicago: American Library Association, 1987.

A collection of theme-oriented programs, as well as instructional material for programming geared to two-year-olds.

Opie, Iona, and Peter Opie, eds. *The Oxford Nursery Rhyme Book*. Oxford: Oxford University Press, 1955.

For the Mother-Goose scholar, complete with 800 rhymes and 600 illustrations, a treasure trove of verse and song to celebrate childhood.

_____. *The Oxford Dictionary of Nursery Rhymes*. London: Oxford University Press, 1929.

The definitive source for Mother Goose rhymes, divided, notated, explained.

Ra, Carol R., comp. *Trot, Trot to Boston: Play Rhymes for Baby*. Illus. by Catherine Stock. New York: Lothrop, Lee, & Shepard, 1987.

A charming collection of twenty-two finger plays and lap rhymes in picture-book form with instructions to help the adult reader use them.

Raffi. *The Raffi Singable Songbook*. Illus. by Joyce Yamamoto. New York: Crown Publishers, Inc. 1980.

Some original, some traditional, all singable songs fill this first book by this ever-popular children's entertainer.

_____. *The Second Raffi Songbook.* Illus. by Joyce Yamamoto. New York: Crown Publishers, Inc. 1986.

Selections from three of his albums, done with the recognizable Raffi flavor.

Ring a Ring o' Roses: Stories, Games, and Finger Plays for Children. Flint, Michigan: Flint Public Library, 1971.

A collection, thematically arranged, of songs, games, and finger plays, some of which are accompanied by directions, for use in programs and at home.

Scott, Louise Binder, and J. J. Thompson. *Rhymes for Fingers and Flannelboards.* Illus. by Jean Flowers. New York: McGraw-Hill, 1960.

A wide-ranging, wonderful collection of finger plays, some paired with directions for use with the flannel board, and all perfect for use with babies and young children.

Sharon, Lois and Bram. *Sharon, Lois, and Bram's Mother Goose: Songs, Finger Rhymes, Tickling Verses, and Games and More.* Illus. by Maryann Kovalski. Boston: The Atlantic Monthly Press, 1985.

These are all done with the energy and style distinctly belonging to Sharon, Lois, and Bram, with charming illustrations and decorations.

Sutherland, Zena, comp. *The Orchard Book of Nursery Rhymes.* Illus. by Faith Jacques. New York: Orchard Books, 1990.

An extensive collection of old and new nursery rhymes, all illustrated in a delicate, old-fashioned style.

Stangl, Jean. *Paper Stories.* Illus. by Walt Shelly. Belmont, Calif.: David S. Lake Publishers, 1984.

A collection of thirty-one original stories and poems for young children with easy-to-cut paper illustrations that are both simple and fun.

Stevenson, Burton Egbert. *The Home Book of Verse for Young Folks.* Illus. by Willy Pogany. New York: Holt, Rinehart and Winston, Inc.

A chapter titled "In the Nursery" opens this delightfully old-fashioned collection of verse.

Warren, Jean, comp. *More Piggyback Songs.* Illus. by Marion Hopping Ekberg. Everett, Wash.: Warren Publishing House, 1984.

A continuation of the Piggyback song series in which new words are set to familiar childhood tunes.

_____. *Piggyback Songs for Infants and Toddlers.* Illus. by Marion Hopping Ekberg. Everett, Wash.: Warren Publishing House, 1985.

New lyrics for familiar tunes suited to situations familiar to very young children—helping around the house, holidays, etc.

Yolen, Jane, ed. *The Lullaby Songbook*. Illus. by Charles Mikolaycak; musical arrangements by Adam Stemple. San Diego: Harcourt Brace Jovanovich, 1986.

   A collection of fifteen soft and soothing lullabies, each with an historic note and a musical arrangement.

_____. *The Laptime Song and Play Book*. Illus. by Margot Tomes; musical arrangements by Adam Stemple. New York: Harcourt Brace Jovanovich, 1989.

   Sixteen gems for adults to sing, say, and share with babies they love.

Mother

Goose

Time

Rhyme Index Section

For convenience in finding rhymes, several types of rhyme indexes are provided. First, a title index includes all rhymes. The second index lists spoken and sung rhymes separately. Then, Lap rhymes are divided into three sets by the developmental group for which they are appropriate: Lap rhymes for both groups; Lap rhymes for Prewalkers only; Lap rhymes for Walkers only. Imitation and Activity rhymes are sorted in the same manner in the following two indexes. Occasionally, a category of rhymes will not appear in a certain developmental group. For example, there are no Lap rhymes designated for Walkers only. The final index in this section is a first-line index.

Title Index
of All Rhymes
and Songs

(Musical arrangement for Sung Rhymes indicated by second page number.)

All the Pretty Little Horses   69, 107
April Month Rhyme   65
August Month Rhyme   66

Baa, Baa, Black Sheep   61
Baby A-Go Go   44, 107
Bees Do Not Like the Snow   59
Bend and Stretch   102, 108
Big A   51
Blue Bird, Blue Bird   94, 108

Catch a Wee Mouse   42
Chin Chopper   55
Clap Hands   51, 108
Clap, Clap, Clap Your Hands   100, 108
Colors Game   96
Come a Look a See   77, 109

December Month Rhyme   66
Diddle Diddle Dumpling   57
Down by the Station   91, 109

Eensy Weensy Spider   85
Exercises   91

Fe, Fi, Fo, Fum   73
February Month Rhyme   65
Five Kittens in the Bed   85, 109
Five Little Monkeys   80, 110
Five Little Pumpkins   79, 110
Five Little Fingers   52
Five Plump Peas   82
Flying Man   43

German Game   89
Grandma's Glasses   78
Green Leaf   84

Head, Shoulders, Knees and Toes   97, 111
Heads, Shoulders, Knees and Toes in French   87
Hello Song   71, 111
Hello Song II   71, 111
Here is a Bunny   84
Here is a Doughnut   48
Here is the Beehive   80
Here Sits the Lord Mayor   55
Here Stands a Redbird   94, 112
Here's a Cup   82
Hey Diddle Diddle   59, 112
Hickety Pickety   65
Hickory Dickory Dock   60, 112
Higglety Pigglety Pop   59
Hot Cross Buns   61, 113
Humpty Dumpty   62, 113
Hush Little Baby   70

I Eat My Peas with Honey   57
I Have a Little Heart   98
I Have Ten Fingers   76
I Hear Thunder   77
I Put My Arms Up High   102
I Saw a Little Rabbit   80

I Wiggle My Fingers   75
If You're Happy and You Know It   96, 114
If Your Fingers   47
I'm Growing   102, 114
It's Raining, It's Pouring   62

Jack and Jill   61
Jack Be Nimble   43
Jack Sprat   64
Jack-O-Lantern   49
Jack-O-Lantern II   49
January Month Rhyme   65
Japanese Game   86
July Month Rhyme   66
June Month Rhyme   66

Lavender's Blue   69, 115
Leg Over Leg   44
Little Baby Dear   102, 115
Little Bo Peep   64
Little Boy Blue   63, 116
Little Brown Seed   95
Little Jack Horner   64, 116
Little Leaves   95
Little Miss Muffet   60
Little Snowboy   55
Little Teapot   96
London Bridge   68

March Month Rhyme   65
Marching Song   92
Mary Had A Little Lamb   64
Mary Had A Little Lamb - Exercise   52
Mary, Mary, Quite Contrary   63
May Month Rhyme   66
Mister Sun   94, 117
Mother and Father and Uncle John   45

Mulberry Bush   92
My Eyes Can See   72
Myself   72

Noble Duke of York   90, 117
November Month Rhyme   66

October Month Rhyme   66
Oh, Baby   45, 118
Old King Cole   58
Old MacDonald   60
Old Mother Goose   59, 118
Once I Saw a Little Bird   84
One Potato   52
One, Two, Buckle My Shoe   62
Open, Shut Them   73, 119

Pancake   84
Pat A Cake   48
Pease Porridge Hot   78
Peter, Peter Pumpkin Eater   61
Pig-A-Wig   42
Pitter Patter   78
Polly Put the Kettle On   58, 119
Pussy Cat, Pussy Cat   58
Put Your Finger On Your Shirt   74
Put Your Finger On Your Nose   75

Quiet-Time Rhyme   98

Rain on the Rooftops   48
Rain, Rain Go Away   48, 120
Rickety Rickety Rocking Horse   43
Ride a Cock Horse   45, 120
Riding Game   53
Rigadoon   44
Ring Around the Rosie   95

Rock A Bye Baby   69
Roll Your Hands   99
Rooster Crows   60
Round and Round the Garden   45
Round Ball   51
Rub A Dub Dub   49

Sat a Little Hare   42
See Saw Margery Daw   68
September Month Rhyme   66
Shoe the Old Horse   42
Simple Simon   56
Sing a Song of Sixpence   62
Sing With Me   98
Snowman   95
Sometimes I Am Tall   99
Spanish Chocolate Rhyme   87
Star Light Star Bright   66
Stoplight   57

Teddy Bear, Teddy Bear   93
Thank You Rhyme   71
These Are Baby's Fingers   44
They're A Part of Me   76
This Is My Garden   79
This Little Pig   47
Three Wise Men of Gotham   63
Tickle On Knee   51
To Market, To Market   54, 120
Tommy O'Flynn   43
Touch Your Head   72
Touch Your Nose   46
Trot, Trot to Boston   47
Twinkle, Twinkle Little Star   68
Two by Two   92, 120
Two Little Blackbirds   81
Two Little Feet   100

Up, Up, Up   90, 121

Valentines   47

Wash the Dishes   78
What Are You Wearing?   46
Wheels on the Bus   82, 121
Where Is Thumbkins   73
Wiggle, Wiggle Fingers   75
With Our Hands   76

Yankee Doodle - Exercise   53

Title Index
of Spoken Rhymes

April Month Rhyme 65
August Month Rhyme 66

Bees Do Not Like the Snow 59
Big A 51

Catch A Wee Mouse 42
Chin Chopper 55

December Month Rhyme 66
Diddle Diddle Dumpling 57

Exercises 91

Fe, Fi, Fo, Fum 73
February Month Rhyme 65
Five Little Fingers 52
Five Plump Peas 82
Flying Man 43

German Game 89
Grandma's Glasses 78
Green Leaf 84

Here Is A Bunny 84
Here Is A Doughnut 48
Here Is The Beehive 80

Here Sits the Lord Mayor   55
Here's A Cup   82
Hickety Pickety   65
Higglety Pigglety Pop   59

I Eat My Peas With Honey   57
I Have A Little Heart   98
I Have Ten Fingers   76
I Put My Arms Up High   102
I Saw A Little Rabbit   80
If Your Fingers   47

Jack Be Nimble   43
Jack Sprat   64
Jack-O-Lantern   49
Jack-O-Lantern II   49
January Month Rhyme   65
Japanese Game   86
July Month Rhyme   66
June Month Rhyme   66

Leg Over Leg   44
Little Bo Peep   64
Little Brown Seed   95
Little Miss Muffet   60
Little Snowboy   55

March Month Rhyme   65
Mary, Mary, Quite Contrary   63
May Month Rhyme   66
Mother and Father and Uncle John   45
My Eyes Can See   72
Myself   72

November Month Rhyme   66

October Month Rhyme   66
Old King Cole   58
Once I Saw A Little Bird   84
One Potato   52
One, Two, Buckle My Shoe   62

Pancake   84
Pat A Cake   48
Pease Porridge Hot   78
Peter, Peter Pumpkin Eater   61
Pig-A-Wig   42
Pitter Patter   78
Pussy Cat, Pussy Cat   58

Quiet-Time Rhyme   98

Rain on the Rooftops   48
Rickety Rickety Rocking Horse   43
Riding Game   53
Rigadoon   44
Rooster Crows   60
Round and Round the Garden   45
Round Ball   51
Rub a Dub Dub   49

Sat a Little Hare   42
September Month Rhyme   66
Shoe the Old Horse   42
Simple Simon   56
Sometimes I Am Tall   99
Spanish Chocolate Rhyme   87
Star Light Star Bright   66
Stoplight   57

Teddy Bear, Teddy Bear   93
Thank You Rhyme   71

These Are Baby's Fingers   44
This Is My Garden   79
This Little Pig   47
Three Wise Men of Gotham   63
Tickle on Knee   51
Touch Your Head   72
Trot, Trot to Boston   47
Two Little Blackbirds   81

Wash the Dishes   78
Wiggle, Wiggle Fingers   75
With Our Hands   76

Title Index
of Sung Rhymes

(Musical arrangement for Sung Rhymes indicated by second page number.)

All the Pretty Little Horses   69, 107

Baa, Baa, Black Sheep   61
Baby A-Go Go   44, 107
Bend and Stretch   102, 108
Blue Bird, Blue Bird   94, 108

Clap Hands   51, 108
Clap, Clap, Clap Your Hands   100, 108
Colors Game   96
Come A Look A See   77, 109

Down by the Station   91, 109

Eensy Weensy Spider   85

Five Kittens in the Bed   85, 109
Five Little Monkeys   80, 110
Five Little Pumpkins   79, 110

Head, Shoulders, Knees and Toes   97, 111
Heads, Shoulders, Knees and Toes in French   87
Hello Song   71, 111
Hello Song II   71, 111
Here Stands a Redbird   94, 112

Hey Diddle Diddle   59, 112
Hickory Dickory Dock   60, 112
Hot Cross Buns   61, 113
Humpty Dumpty   62, 113
Hush Little Baby   70

I Hear Thunder   77
I Wiggle My Fingers   75
If You're Happy and You Know It   96, 114
I'm Growing   102, 114
It's Raining, It's Pouring   62

Jack and Jill   61

Lavender's Blue   69, 115
Little Baby Dear   102, 115
Little Boy Blue   63, 116
Little Jack Horner   64, 116
Little Leaves   95
Little Teapot   96
London Bridge   68

Marching Song   92
Mary Had A Little Lamb   64
Mary Had A Little Lamb - Exercise   52
Mister Sun   94, 117
Mulberry Bush   92

Noble Duke of York   90, 117

Oh, Baby   45, 118
Old MacDonald   60
Old Mother Goose   59, 118
Open, Shut Them   73, 119

Polly Put the Kettle On   58, 119
Put Your Finger On Your Shirt   74
Put Your Finger On Your Nose   75

Rain, Rain Go Away   48, 120
Ride a Cock Horse   45, 120
Ring Around the Rosie   95
Rock a Bye Baby   69
Roll Your Hands   99

See Saw Margery Daw   68
Sing A Song of Sixpence   62
Sing With Me   98
Snowman   95

They're a Part of Me   76
To Market, To Market   54, 120
Tommy O'Flynn   43
Touch Your Nose   46
Twinkle, Twinkle Little Star   68
Two By Two   92, 120
Two Little Feet   100

Up, Up, Up   90, 121

Valentines   47

What Are You Wearing?   46
Wheels on the Bus   82, 121
Where Is Thumbkins   73

Yankee Doodle - Exercise   53

Title Index
of Rhymes and Songs
by Developmental Levels:
Lap Rhymes, Prewalkers

Baby A-Go Go   44, 107
Big A   51

Catch a Wee Mouse   42
Chin Chopper   55

Five Little Fingers   52
Flying Man   43

Here Sits the Lord Mayor   55
Hey Diddle Diddle   59, 112
Higglety Pigglety Pop   59

Jack Be Nimble   43

Lavender's Blue   69, 115
Leg Over Leg   44

Mary Had A Little Lamb - Exercise   52
Mother and Father and Uncle John   45

Old Mother Goose   59, 118
One Potato   52

Pig-A-Wig   42

Rickety Rickety Rocking Horse   43
Ride a Cock Horse   45, 120
Rigadoon   44
Rooster Crows   60
Round Ball   51

Sat a Little Hare   42
See Saw Margery Daw   68
Shoe the Old Horse   42
Star Light Star Bright   66

These Are Baby's Fingers   44
To Market, To Market   54, 120
Tommy O'Flynn   43
Trot, Trot to Boston   47

Yankee Doodle - Exercise   53

Lap Rhymes, Both Groups

All the Pretty Little Horses   69, 107
April Month Rhyme   65
August Month Rhyme   66

Baa, Baa, Black Sheep   61
Bees Do Not Like the Snow   59

Clap Hands   51, 108
Come a Look a See   77, 109

December Month Rhyme   66
Diddle Diddle Dumpling   57

February Month Rhyme   65

Here Is A Doughnut   48
Hickety Pickety   65
Hickory Dickory Dock   60, 112
Hot Cross Buns   61, 113
Humpty Dumpty   62, 113
Hush Little Baby   70

I Eat My Peas With Honey   57
If Your Fingers   47
It's Raining, It's Pouring   62

Jack and Jill   61
Jack Sprat   64
Jack-O-Lantern   49

Jack-O-Lantern II   49
January Month Rhyme   65
July Month Rhyme   66
June Month Rhyme   66

Little Bo Peep   64
Little Boy Blue   63, 116
Little Jack Horner   64, 116
Little Miss Muffet   60
Little Snowboy   55
London Bridge   68

March Month Rhyme   65
Mary Had A Little Lamb   64
Mary, Mary, Quite Contrary   63
May Month Rhyme   66

November Month Rhyme   66

October Month Rhyme   66
Oh, Baby   45, 118
Old King Cole   58
Old MacDonald   60
One, Two, Buckle My Shoe   62

Pat A Cake   48
Peter, Peter Pumpkin Eater   61
Polly Put the Kettle On   58, 119
Pussy Cat, Pussy Cat   58

Rain on the Rooftops   48
Rain, Rain Go Away   48, 120
Riding Game   53
Rock A Bye Baby   69
Round and Round the Garden   45
Rub a Dub Dub   49

September Month Rhyme   66
Simple Simon   56
Sing a Song of Sixpence   62
Stoplight   57

This Little Pig   47
Three Wise Men of Gotham   63
Tickle on Knee   51
Touch Your Nose   46
Twinkle, Twinkle Little Star   68

Valentines   47

What Are You Wearing?   46

Imitation Rhymes, Walkers

Eensy Weensy Spider   85

Fe, Fi, Fo, Fum   73
Five Kittens in the Bed   85, 109
Five Little Monkeys   80, 110
Five Little Pumpkins   79, 110

German Game   89
Green Leaf   84

Here is a Bunny   84

I Hear Thunder   77
I Saw a Little Rabbit   80
I Wiggle My Fingers   75

Japanese Game   86

Once I Saw a Little Bird   84

Pancake   84
Pitter Patter   78

Spanish Chocolate Rhyme   87

They're a Part of Me   76
This is My Garden   79

Wash the Dishes   78
Wheels on the Bus   82, 121
Where is Thumbkins   73
With Our Hands   76

Imitation Rhymes, Both Groups

Five Plump Peas   82

Grandma's Glasses   78

Hello Song   71, 111
Hello Song II   71, 111
Here Is the Beehive   80
Here's a Cup   82

I Have Ten Fingers   76

My Eyes Can See   72
Myself   72

Open, Shut Them   73, 119

Pease Porridge Hot   78
Put Your Finger On Your Shirt   74
Put Your Finger On Your Nose   75

Thank You Rhyme   71
Touch Your Head   72
Two Little Blackbirds   81

Wiggle, Wiggle Fingers   75

Activity Rhymes, Walkers

Bend and Stretch   102, 108
Blue Bird, Blue Bird   94, 108

Clap, Clap, Clap Your Hands   100, 108
Colors Game   96

Down by the Station   91, 109

Head, Shoulders, Knees and Toes   97, 111
Heads, Shoulders, Knees and Toes in French   87
Here Stands a Redbird   94, 112

I Have a Little Heart   98
I Put My Arms Up High   102
If You're Happy and You Know It   96, 114
I'm Growing   102, 114

Little Baby Dear   102, 115
Little Brown Seed   95
Little Leaves   95
Little Teapot   96

Marching Song   92
Mister Sun   94, 117
Mulberry Bush   92

Quiet-Time Rhyme   98

Ring Around the Rosie   95
Roll Your Hands   99

Sing With Me   98
Snowman   95
Sometimes I Am Tall   99

Teddy Bear, Teddy Bear   93
Two By Two   92, 120
Two Little Feet   100

Activity Rhymes, Both Groups

Exercises   91

Noble Duke of York   90, 117

Up, Up, Up   90, 121

First Line Index
of All Rhymes

(Name) has a (color) shirt on   46
A face so round   49
A trot, and a canter   44
April brings the primrose sweet   65
Arms up high above the head   53
August brings the sheaves of corn   66

Baa, baa black sheep   61
Baby a-go go   44
Bees do not like the snow   59
Bend and stretch so way up high   102
Big A   51
Blue bird, blue bird   94

Carve a jack-o-lantern   49
Chill December brings the sleet   66
Clap, clap, clap your hands   100
Clap hands, clap hands   51
Clap your hands, little Baby   102
Clap your hands, now   76
Come a look a see   77
Come along and sing with me   98

Diddle, diddle, dumpling, my son John   57
Down by the station   91
Dull November brings the blast   66

Eins, zwei, Polizei   89
Exercises, exercises   91

Fe, fi, fo, fum   73
February brings the rain   65
Five kittens in the bed   85
Five little fingers on this hand   52
Five little monkeys   80
Five little pumpkins   79
Five plump peas   82
Flying man, flying man   43
Fresh October brings the pheasant   66

Hana, hana, hana kuchi   86
Head, shoulders, knees and toes   97
Hello everybody   71
Hello, hello   71
Here is a bunny   84
Here is a doughnut   48
Here is the beehive   80
Here sits the Lord Mayor   55
Here stands a redbird   94
Here we go up, up, up   90
Here we go round the mulberry bush   92
Here's a cup   82
Here's a green leaf   84
Hey diddle, diddle   59
Hickety, pickety, my black hen   65
Hickory, dickory dock   60
Higglety pigglety pop   59
Hot cross buns   61
Hot July brings cooling showers   66
Humpty Dumpty sat on a wall   62
Hush, little baby, don't say a word   70
Hush-a-bye, don't you cry   69

I eat my peas with honey   57
I have a little heart   98
I have ten fingers   76
I hear thunder, I hear thunder   77
I put my arms up high   102
I saw a little rabbit   80
I wiggle my fingers   75
I'll touch my hair   98
I'm a little teapot   96
I'm a little brown seed   95
I'm growing, I'm growing   102
If you are a lady/gentleman   51
If you have a (color) shirt on   96
If you're happy and you know it   96
If your fingers wiggle   47
It's raining, it's pouring   62

Jack and Jill went up the hill   61
Jack be nimble   43
Jack Sprat could eat no fat   64
January brings the snow   65
June brings tulips, lilies, roses   66

Knock on the door   55

Lavender's blue, dilly dilly   69
Leg over leg   44
Legs apart   52
Let's march together   92
Little Bo Peep has lost her sheep   64
Little Boy Blue   63
Little Jack Horner   64
Little leaves fall   95
Little Miss Muffet   60
London bridge is falling down   68

March brings breezes, loud and shrill   65
Mary had a little lamb   52
Mary had a little lamb   64
Mary, Mary, quite contrary   63
May brings flocks of pretty lambs   66
Mix a pancake, stir a pancake   84
Mother and Father and Uncle John   45
My eyes can see   72

Oh Mister Sun, Sun   94
Oh, the noble Duke of York   90
Old King Cole was a merry old soul   58
Old MacDonald had a farm, e-i-e-i-o   60
Old Mother Goose   59
On my face I have a nose   72
Once I saw a little bird   84
One, two, buckle my shoe   62
One, two, three   60
Open, shut them, open, shut them   73
Our hands say thank you   71

Pat a cake, pat a cake   48
Pease porridge hot   78
Peter, Peter pumpkin eater   61
Pitter patter falls the rain   78
Polly put the kettle on   58
Pussy cat, pussy cat   58
Put your finger on your shirt   74
Put your finger on your nose   75

Rain on the rooftops   48
Rain, rain go away   48
Red says stop   57
Rickety, rickety rocking horse   43
Ride a cock horse to Banbury Cross   45
Ring around the rosie   95
Rock a bye baby   69

Roll him and roll him   95
Roll, roll, roll your hands   99
Round about, round about   42
Round and round the garden   45
Round ball, round ball   51
Rub a dub dub   49

Say, say oh, baby   45
See saw Margery Daw   68
September blows soft   66
Shoe the old horse   42
Simple Simon met a pieman   56
Sing a song of sixpence   62
Sometimes I am tall   99
Star light, star bright   66

Teddy Bear, Teddy Bear   93
Tete, epaules, genoux et pieds   87
The eensy weensy spider   85
The wheels on the bus   82
These are baby's fingers   44
These are Grandma's glasses   78
This is my garden   79
This is the way the farmer rides   53
This little pig went to market   47
This little pig had a rub-a-dub   42
Three wise men of Gotham   63
To market to market   54
Tommy O'Flynn and his old gray mare   43
Touch your head   72
Touch your nose, touch your chin   46
Trot, trot to Boston   47
Twinkle, twinkle little star   68
Two little blackbirds   81
Two little feet go tap tap tap   100

Uno, dos, tres cho   87

Valentines, valentines   47

Walking along two by two   92
Warm September brings the fruit   66
Wash the dishes   78
We make one little snowboy   55
Where is Thumbkins   73
Wiggle, wiggle fingers   75
With our hands   76